THE GR

MW00795460

Trekking the
WEST
HIGHLAND
WAY

by
Andrew
McCluggage

KNIFE
EDGE
Outdoor Guidebooks

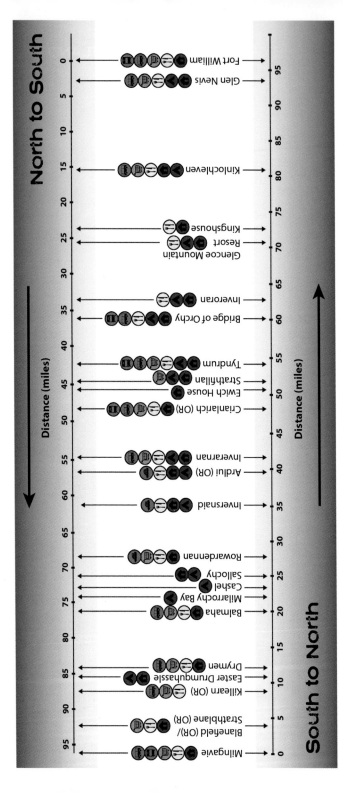

North to South

Distance (miles)

Fort William	0
Glen Nevis	
Kinlochleven	15
Kingshouse	
Glencoe Mountain Resort	25
Inveroran	
Bridge of Orchy	35
Tyndrum	
Strathfillan	45
Ewich House	
Crianlarich (OR)	
Inverarnan	55
Ardlui (OR)	
Inversnaid	
Rowardennan	
Sallochy	
Cashel	
Milarrchy Bay	
Balmaha	
Drymen	
Easter Drumquhassle	
Killearn (OR)	
Blanefield (OR)/ Strathblane (OR)	
Milngavie	

South to North

Distance (miles)

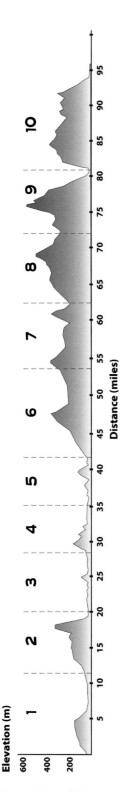

Elevation (m)

600
400
200

1   2   3   4   5   6   7   8   9   10

Distance (miles)

5   10   15   20   25   30   35   40   45   50   55   60   65   70   75   80   85   90   95

🔵 **Accommodation:** B&B, pub/inn, hostel, bunkhouse and/or hotel

🔺 **Campsite**

🍴 **Food:** pub, restaurant and/or café serving lunch and/or dinner

🏢 **Shop or supermarket selling food or groceries**

🚌 **Bus services:** may not be daily

🚆 **Train services**

⛴ **Ferry or water-taxi service**

Note: It is not possible to list all of the locations with facilities in the diagram. Only key locations are shown.

Ask the Author

If you have any questions which are not answered by this book, then you can ask the author on our Facebook group, 'West Highland Way Q&A'. The group's URL is **www.facebook.com/groups/WestHighlandWayTrek**

About the Author

Andrew McCluggage is an outdoor writer and photographer from Northern Ireland. After 20 years as a corporate lawyer, he decided to do something interesting and started writing walking guidebooks.

His first book was Walking in the Briançonnais, covering a beautiful part of the French Alps. Since then, he has written a variety of guidebooks for hiking and trekking.

Other Knife Edge Outdoor Guidebooks written by Andrew include:

► **Trekking the Hadrian's Wall Path**

► **Trekking the South Downs Way**

► **Northern Ireland: The Unmissable Walks**

► **The Mourne Mountains**

► **Tour du Mont Blanc**

► **Trekking the Dolomites AV1**

► **Walker's Haute Route: Chamonix to Zermatt**

► **Trekking the Corsica GR20**

► **Walking Chamonix-Mont Blanc**

► **Walking Brittany**

► **Tour of the Écrins National Park (GR54)**

► **Big Hikes in the Mourne Mountains**

e old military road to
idge of Orchy (Stage 7a)

Key for Route Maps

 S F Start/Finish of Stage   (1) Waypoint

 Wild Campsite   Train Station

7 Accommodation

N   0   1km

Publisher: Knife Edge Outdoor Limited (NI648568)
12 Torrent Business Centre, Donaghmore, County Tyrone, BT70 3BF, UK
www.knifeedgeoutdoor.com

©Andrew McCluggage 2022
All photographs: ©Andrew McCluggage 2022
ISBN: 978-1-912933-11-2

First edition 2022

A catalogue record for this book is available from the British Library.

Map on inside cover: ©Knife Edge Outdoor Limited
Other maps: ©Crown Copyright and database rights 2022
OS 100063385

Front cover: view of Beinn Dòrain (Stage 7a)
Title page: descending towards Glencoe Mountain Resort (Stage 8a)
This page: Loch Lomond (Stage 3d)

All routes described in this guide have been recently walked by the author a
both the author and publisher have made all reasonable efforts to ensure tl
all information is as accurate as possible. However, while a printed book rema
constant for the life of an edition, things in the countryside often change. Tra
are subject to forces outside our control. For example, landslides, tree-falls or otl
matters can result in damage to paths or route changes; waymarks and signpo
may fade or be destroyed by wind, snow or the passage of time; or trails may r
be maintained by the relevant authorities. If you notice any discrepancies betwe
the contents of this guide and the facts on the ground, then please let us know. C
contact details are listed at the back of this book

ontents

Glen Falloch (Stage 6

Getting Help

Emergency services number: dial 999

Distress signal

The signal that you are in distress is 6 blasts on a whistle spaced over a minute, followed by a minute's silence. Then repeat. The acknowledgment that your signal has been received is 3 blasts of a whistle over a minute followed by a minute's silence. At night, flashes of a torch can also be used in the same sequences. **Always carry a torch and whistle.**

Signalling to a helicopter from the ground

Help Required

Raise both arms in the shape of a 'Y'

Help Not Required

Raise one arm and extend the other arm down and outwards

WARNING

Hills, cliffs and mountains can be dangerous places and walking is a potentially dangerous activity. Many of the routes described in this guide cross exposed and potentially hazardous terrain. You walk entirely at your own risk. It is solely your responsibility to ensure that you and all members of your group have adequate experience, fitness and equipment. Neither the author nor the publisher accepts any responsibility or liability whatsoever for death, injury, loss, damage or inconvenience resulting from use of this book, participation in the activity of mountain walking or otherwise.

Some land may be privately owned so we cannot guarantee that there is a legal right of entry to the land. Occasionally, routes change as a result of land disputes.

Climbing to Cnap (Stage 5b)

...ic Hill and Loch Lomond (Stage 2b)

...British countryside is spectacular and varied and so it is no surprise that Great Britain ...cked with avid hikers. The right to access the countryside is enshrined in law and ...e are countless paths and tracks which are open to walkers. These paths and tracks, ... created many centuries ago, enable the hiker to travel through some of the wildest ...most beautiful terrain that Europe has to offer. And rarely is that terrain wilder or more ...tiful than the landscape of Scotland, the most unpopulated and remote part of GB. ...mote that even the Romans (whose empire stretched from Britain all the way to what ...w Turkey) were unable to conquer it in any meaningful respect.

...it is within that wild and remote terrain that you will find the West Highland Way ...W') which travels 96 miles through sublime scenery, from the outskirts of Glasgow ...rt William. In between, there are countless magnificent mountains, exquisite glens, ...mering lochs and seemingly endless miles of purple heather to experience. The WHW ...er negotiates this wonderfully unpopulated terrain on a meticulously waymarked ...s of paths and tracks, many of which are historic military roads or drovers' paths. In ...art of the Highlands, you are far away from urban centres. Occasionally, you will meet ...d or pass through a small village or hamlet (with little more than a local pub and a ...laces to stay) but otherwise, the experience is one of tranquillity. This is Scotland at ...st and it will be an adventure that you will never forget.

...VHW was officially opened in 1980 and it was Scotland's first official long-distance ... Today, it is one of Scotland's official national trails known as 'Scotland's Great Trails'. It ...miles (155km) in length with approximately 10,700ft (3,300m) of ascent and descent. ...ighest point on the trail is the Devil's Staircase (548m). If those statistics sound ...idating then do not worry: with the right preparation, planning and approach, the ...' is perfectly manageable for most people of reasonable fitness. Yes, it is a challenge ...is an achievable one. And that is where this book comes in! Most of what you need ...ow to plan, and prepare for, the WHW is here within these pages and the entire route ...cribed in detail to guide you on the trek itself. Furthermore, unlike some other books, ...ne contains real Ordnance Survey maps: for each stage, there are 1:25,000 scale ...to go with the accurate and concise route descriptions. Because all the maps are set ...ithin the guidebook itself, there is no need to fumble about with a guidebook in one ...and a map in the other.

We aim to ensure that you will have the best chance possible of completing the trek. place great importance on the correct preparation and we focus in detail on moc lightweight equipment (see 'Equipment'). We also believe that it is crucial to match y itinerary to your experience, fitness and ability. Accordingly, we have included here extraordinary level of detail on itinerary planning: our unique itinerary planner ha different itineraries to choose from. For each itinerary, we have completed for you all difficult calculations of time, distance and altitude gain/loss. This makes it easy for yo design a manageable itinerary that fits your specific needs. Once on the trail, you wi able to relax and fully enjoy one of the world's great treks.

How hard is the WHW?

Notwithstanding the challenges, it is estimated that tens of thousands of hikers walk full length of the WHW each year. It is therefore an achievable endeavour. However, e day you will need to walk a significant distance across undulating terrain so a reason level of fitness is required. That said, the WHW has much less climbing and descend than many other treks and it is considered to be one of the easiest multi-day hikes ir UK. In fact, there are only about 10,700ft (3,300m) of ascent and descent on the entire and these are relatively well spread out across the length of the route.

For the most part, the WHW uses clear paths and tracks which are simple to negot There are also some short sections along minor roads. The route is well marked. I people walk the WHW in six to ten days. However, fit and experienced hikers can finish five days and endurance runners often do it even faster. Others prefer to walk more sl and spend 11 days soaking up all of the delights on offer, lingering over packed lun whilst savouring the magnificent views, and enjoying the beer in the country pubs a the way. There is plenty of accommodation on, or near, the trail so it is simple to plan distances to suit your requirements.

Direction and start/finish points

The WHW runs between Milngavie (on the outskirts of Glasgow) in the S and Fort Wi in the N. You can hike it in either direction so this book describes both approaches in However, there are some compelling reasons for hiking S-N. Firstly, it is preferable to the trek with the least challenging stage and finish with the hardest ones. Section the S end of the trek (between Milngavie and Drymen) is probably the easiest part c WHW and is therefore a sensible first stage, giving your body a more gentle introdu to the trail. And Section 10, at the N end (between Kinlochleven and Fort Willia arguably the most challenging part of the WHW: the route is long, the terrain undu relentlessly and it has to be completed in one day as there is no accommodation section to break up the journey. Accordingly, it is preferable to walk Section 10 at the of the trek when you are 'trail-hardened' rather than at the start of it when your leg not yet have become accustomed to the rigours of daily walking. S-N trekkers will f easier to plan a balanced route, starting with short slow days and gradually increasin difficulty. N-S hikers, on the other hand, must begin with the difficult Section 10, wi the opportunity to warm-up first on easier parts of the trail.

Secondly, the views on Sections 8, 9 and 10 (as you approach the mighty Ben Nevi highest mountain in the UK) are some of the finest on the WHW and for S-N hikers a epic climax to a wonderful journey. N-S trekkers, on the other hand, will experience key attractions during the first few days (before they have found rhythm and fitnes will be less able to relax and enjoy the scenic delights. Furthermore, N-S trekkers will their trek on the lowlands approaching Glasgow which is a much less euphoric end t

...he world's great treks than the sight of Ben Nevis. In fact, it is arguable that the scenery
...he WHW improves gradually all the way from S to N, delivering up incrementally more
...ly views day by day.

...his book, we cater for both N-S and S-N trekkers: route descriptions and a variety of
...raries are given for each approach. The numbered waypoints on the real maps make
...route simple to follow in either direction.

...king shorter sections of the WHW

...king the WHW in one go is a wonderful experience but there are other ways to enjoy
...incredible trail. If you do not wish to walk the entire route, it is possible to walk shorter
...ions of it. There are numerous escape/access points along the route where you could
...e or join the trek using public transport or taxis: see 'Secondary trail-heads'. You could
...' at any of these places and walk a few sections. Or you could skip sections by leaving
...oute at one of these points.

...hermore, many people prefer to hike the WHW in day-long sections using public
...sport to travel to/from the start and finish points: see 'Public transport along the
...V'. Over the course of months or years, they will eventually complete the entire trek.
...y others have no desire to walk the WHW in its entirety and simply want to experience
...v of its highlights. The Itinerary Planner should help you to plan day-walks along the
...V. Often day-walkers hike in groups, leaving a car at each end of their route.

...uided tours, self-guided tours or
...dependent walking?

...quently asked question is whether to walk independently or with an organised
...p. The answer is a personal one, depending upon your own particular circumstances
...equirements. For many, the decision to organise the trek themselves, and to walk
...pendently, can be almost life-changing, opening the door for other challenges in
...uture. There is much satisfaction to be gained from planning and navigating a trek
...self and the sense of achievement on completion is to be savoured.

...ever, the independent trekker usually carries a full pack and is responsible for all daily
...ions such as pacing, which way to go at junctions, when to stock up with food/water
...hoice of route in bad weather. For some, this will be too great a burden on top of
...hysical effort required simply to walk the route. For those walkers, a guided group
...reat solution: the tour company typically organises food, accommodation and (if
...ble) transfer of luggage each night. And the guide makes all the decisions, enabling
...alker to concentrate on the walking. There are many tour companies operating
...d trips on the WHW but you should check whether they cover the full official route
...t some of the highlights.

...uided tours are much more popular and are a sensible middle-ground. The tour
...any books all the accommodation and provides all the advice and information
...ed to complete the trek. However, you will walk the trail without a guide. Normally,
...breakfast will be provided and you can request packed lunches. For evening meals,
...vill usually provide details of pubs and restaurants which are walking distance from
...accommodation. Often, they can transfer your baggage to your accommodation
...ight so you only need to carry a small day-pack on the trail.

...are also some businesses offering accommodation booking services only (such
...erpa Van: see 'Baggage transfer'). And there are businesses that can provide daily

baggage transfer for those who want to walk independently but do not wish to c
heavy bags: see 'Baggage transfer'.

In fact, these days there are so many self-guided tour companies and accommoda
booking services that some of the accommodation along the WHW is block-boc
months in advance. At peak times, this makes it harder for the independent trekke
secure first choice accommodation unless booked well in advance. As a result, m
confident trekkers (who would be perfectly capable of walking independently) bo
self-guided trip simply to avail of the accommodation booking service. By booking a
guided tour or using an accommodation booking service, much of the hassle of plan
the trek is alleviated, albeit at a price.

When to go

The main trekking season runs from Easter to October. Before Easter and after Octo
some accommodation will be closed. The weather in Britain is notoriously wet an
Scotland, the most northerly part of GB, the rain is legendary. Accordingly, you sh
prepare for some wet weather on the WHW, irrespective of the season. That is not to
that it always rains: it is just that statistics dictate that there is a good chance that
will happen at some point along your trek. That said, some seasons are statistically
than others and you can at least attempt to maximise your chances of good weathe
selecting a drier month.

However, weather is not the only consideration because, on the WHW, the infar
Scottish midge makes a regular appearance (see 'Midges'): many trekkers who
experienced a midge attack on a fine and windless summer day will readily attest
a windy, wet day without midges would have been preferable. Furthermore, the \
is a popular trek and can get very busy in high summer, making accommodation
difficult to find than hens' teeth: for some, the volume of trekkers on the trail and
availability of accommodation will be key considerations.

The relative merits of each season are discussed below in detail but, taking all the fa
into consideration, in our opinion, the optimal periods for walking the WHW are mid
to mid-June and the month of September.

Spring (March to May): this can be the most beautiful time of year for walking.
wild-flowers are on show and the gorse will also be in full bloom with its vivid y
flowers and coconut aroma. By May, new growth will be upon the deciduous plant
grass is at its greenest. Of course, rain is a possibility in spring but it usually bec
drier as the season progresses. Indeed, the weather is often sunny and warm and
can be the finest month in Scotland: in recent years, the weather in May has tend
be more favourable than in July and August. Visibility in spring is generally excelle
views are wide-ranging. Early in spring, the number of walkers is lower (except at E
gradually increasing throughout the season. Normally, the midges only start to ma
appearance at the end of May and they are unlikely to be found in the vast quantitie
plague the summer months.

Summer (June to August): this is the peak walking season and visitor numbe
at their greatest. The trails are busy and accommodation is hard to find. The days are
and statistically, your chances of good weather are highest in this period: often June
best month and August is frequently more unsettled. Temperatures are at their pea
there is sometimes haze. This is the worst period for midges which can drive camp
the verges of insanity.

utumn (September to November): although visitor numbers reduce, September is a busy month on the WHW. As soon as the children return to school, retired folk and se without kids come out to play. Autumn often provides excellent walking conditions: weather in September and October can be more settled, with less rain, than in summer. nperatures are lower but still comfortable. Skies can be very clear giving excellent bility and the quality of the low light is magnificent. The wide variety of deciduous nts in the UK means that the autumn colours are stunning. However, as the days get rter, it is wise to start walking early. If something were to go wrong, you would have daylight in which to seek help than in summer. By September, the midges are on decline and the situation improves throughout the season. The weather in November ds to be less conducive to pleasant walking and some accommodation will close.

nter (December to February): these are the coldest months and rain and snow common. A light sprinkling of snow can be a delight for a suitably-equipped walker ough care should be taken. However, walking in deep snow is best left to those with appropriate winter experience and the correct equipment. Even if there is no snow, ch out for ice which forms in places where water collects. Cold months often bring , clear weather and the low sun makes the light very beautiful. A sunny day in winter be one of the best of the year. Days are short so start early. Much accommodation will losed. A winter assault on the WHW is for hardy and experienced hikers only.

Season	Pros	Cons
Spring	Pleasant temperatures Frequent sunny skies Good visibility Gorse and wild-flowers Fewer visitors Normally midge-free	Rainy spells are common in March and April Ground can be wet
Summer	Best chance of fine weather Ground is often dry	Sometimes hazy August sometimes wet Visitor numbers highest Midges are most active
Autumn	Pleasant temperatures Frequent sunny skies Excellent visibility Fewer visitors Normally midge-free Autumn colours	Shorter days Cooler evenings Rainy spells
Winter	Sometimes crisp clear skies Excellent visibility Fewer visitors No midges	Shortest days Can be cold and icy Occasionally, there is snow

Using this book

This book is designed to be used by walkers of differing abilities. Many guidebooks long-distance treks rigidly divide the route into a fixed number of long day stages, leav it up to the walker to break down those stages to design daily routes which suit his/ abilities. This book, however, has been laid out differently to give the trekker flexibilit divides the route into 22 shorter stages which you can combine to design daily routes t meet your own specific needs.

Each of the 22 stages covers the distance between one accommodation option and subsequent one. Most accommodation options on the route are the start/finish poin a stage. You can choose how many of these stages you wish to walk each day. Each st has its own walk description, route map and elevation profile.

The labelling of the stages uses a combination of numbers and letters. It is a simple sys but requires a little bit of explanation. Firstly, we have divided the route into ten 'Secti (numbered from 1 to 10 from S-N): each Section represents one day of our standard day schedule. Within each Section, the route is broken down into stages: every stag labelled with a number between 1 and 10, representing the relevant Section that stage is part of. Every stage is also labelled with a letter. So, for example, the first stag Section 3 would be 'Stage 3a', the next stage would be 'Stage 3b' and so on. Take a loc the detailed Itinerary Planner below and all should become clear.

The Itinerary Planner includes a range of tables outlining 17 suggested itineraries of 3, 6, 7, 8, 9, 10 and 11 days. We include itineraries for both N-S and S-N walkers. In each ta the maths have been done for you so there is no need for you to waste time (and me strength!) working out daily distances, timings and height gain.

Of course, the suggested itineraries are only suggestions. You can shorten or leng your day in any number of ways to suit yourself: just decide how many stages you v to walk that day. It is up to you. As there is accommodation near the end of each stag is easy to design your own bespoke itinerary and adjust it on the ground as you go al

For example, day 6 of our standard 10-day itinerary involves walking Stages 6a, 6b, 6c 6d. But you could decide to extend your day 6 by walking Stages 6a, 6b, 6c, 6d and 7 on the same day. Or you might be tired and decide to shorten your day by walking Stages 6a, 6b and 6c. With some other guidebooks, you would have to work out ho split stages yourself, involving some complicated maths to plan distances and times g forward. This guide, however, does all the hard mental work for you.

In this book:

Timings indicate the approximate time required by a reasonably fit walke complete a stage. They do not include stoppage time. Do not get frustrated if your times do not match ours: everyone walks at different speeds. As you progress throug trek, you will soon learn how your own times compare with those given here and yo adjust your plans accordingly.

Walking distances are given in both miles and kilometres (km). One equates to approximately 1.6km.

ace names in brackets in the route descriptions indicate the direction
e followed on signposts. For example, "('Drymen')" would mean that you follow a sign
Drymen.

cent/descent numbers are the aggregate of all the altitude gain or loss
asured in feet and metres) on the uphill or downhill sections of a stage. As a rule of
mb, a fit walker climbs 1000 to 1300 feet (300 to 400m) in an hour. The ascent/descent
a in the tables in the route descriptions is based on S-N itineraries: N-S walkers should
ply swap the ascent and descent figures.

evation profiles are provided for each Section, indicating where the climbs
descents fall on the route. The profiles are based on S-N itineraries: N-S walkers should
ply read them in reverse.

ellings of place names are normally derived from the OS maps.
vever, there is sometimes disagreement over how places are spelt. Accordingly, you
notice different spellings elsewhere.

al maps are included. These are extracts from 1:25,000 scale Explorer maps
duced by Ordnance Survey, the mapping agency for GB. The maps are divided into
grid squares: each square represents 1km x 1km. On the maps, we have marked
route of the trek, the start/finish points of stages, significant waypoints and all the
ommodation on the WHW. On each map, N is at the top of the page.

e following abbreviations are used:

	Before the Common Era (a secular alternative to 'BC')
	The Common Era (a secular alternative to 'AD')
	Camping Management Zone (see 'Wild camping')
	Great Britain
IP	Loch Lomond & the Trossachs National Park
	Off-route
	Ordnance Survey
C	Scottish Outdoor Access Code
V	The West Highland Way
	Turn left
	Turn right
	Straight ahead
E and W, etc.	North, South, East and West, etc.
	North to South
	South to North

*f Loch Lomond's
beaches (Stage 4)*

Itinerary Planner

South to North

Stage	Start	Time (hr)	Distance		Ascent		Descent	
			miles	km	ft	m	ft	m
1a	Milngavie	4:45	10.9	17.5	446	136	512	1
1b	Easter Drumquhassle	0:15	0.8	1.3	98	30	52	1
2a	Drymen exit	0:15	0.5	0.8	59	18	0	
2b	Glenalva B&B	4:00	7.8	12.5	1253	382	1440	4
3a	Balmaha	0:45	2.0	3.2	171	52	180	5
3b	Milarrochy Bay	0:30	1.3	2.1	98	30	69	2
3c	Cashel	0:45	1.9	3.1	164	50	194	
3d	Sallochy	1:30	2.7	4.3	456	139	417	1
4	Rowardennan	4:00	7.3	11.8	653	199	666	2
5a	Inversnaid	1:45	4.5	7.2	230	70	200	
5b	Ardleish	1:15	2.2	3.5	358	109	404	1
6a	Inverarnan	3:00	6.2	9.9	942	287	164	
6b	Crianlarich exit	1:15	2.6	4.2	463	141	722	2
6c	Ewich House	0:15	1.0	1.6	43	13	16	
6d	Strathfillan	1:00	2.2	3.5	197	60	46	
7a	Tyndrum	2:45	6.5	10.5	364	111	564	1
7b	Bridge of Orchy	1:15	2.5	4.0	535	163	499	1
8a	Inveroran	3:45	8.1	13.1	843	257	400	
8b	Glencoe Mountain Resort exit	0:30	1.3	2.1	33	10	253	
9	Kingshouse	4:30	8.9	14.3	1221	372	2001	
10a	Kinlochleven	6:30	12.9	20.7	2024	617	1887	
10b	Glen Nevis exit	1:00	2.5	4.0	16	5	154	
Finish	Fort William							

Ben Nevis (Stage 10a)

orth to South

tage	Start	Time (hr)	Distance		Ascent		Descent	
			miles	km	ft	m	ft	m
10b	Fort William	1:00	2.5	4.0	154	47	16	5
10a	Glen Nevis exit	6:30	12.9	20.7	1887	575	2024	617
9	Kinlochleven	5:00	8.9	14.3	2001	610	1221	372
8b	Kingshouse	0:45	1.3	2.1	253	77	33	10
8a	Glencoe Mountain Resort exit	3:30	8.1	13.1	400	122	843	257
7b	Inveroran	1:15	2.5	4.0	499	152	535	163
7a	Bridge of Orchy	3:00	6.5	10.5	564	172	364	111
6d	Tyndrum	1:00	2.2	3.5	46	14	197	60
6c	Strathfillan	0:15	1.0	1.6	16	5	43	13
6b	Ewich House	1:30	2.6	4.2	722	220	463	141
6a	Crianlarich exit	2:30	6.2	9.9	164	50	942	287
5b	Inverarnan	1:15	2.2	3.5	404	123	358	109
5a	Ardleish	1:45	4.5	7.2	200	61	230	70
4	Inversnaid	4:00	7.3	11.8	666	203	653	199
3d	Rowardennan	1:30	2.7	4.3	417	127	456	139
3c	Sallochy	0:45	1.9	3.1	194	59	164	50
3b	Cashel	0:30	1.3	2.1	69	21	98	30
3a	Milarrochy Bay	0:45	2.0	3.2	180	55	171	52
2b	Balmaha	4:00	7.8	12.5	1440	439	1253	382
2a	Glenalva B&B	0:15	0.5	0.8	0	0	59	18
1b	Drymen exit	0:15	0.8	1.3	52	16	98	30
1a	Easter Drumquhassle	4:45	10.9	17.5	512	156	446	136
nish	Milngavie							

Suggested Itineraries: South to North

11 Days (S-N)

Our most leisurely itinerary is perfect for those who want to relax and take their ti▮ It is the same as our standard 10-day itinerary except that it also permits an overni▮ stop in Crianlarich. However, the final day is long and tough.

Day	Stages	Time (hr)	Distance miles	Distance km	Ascent ft	Ascent m	Descen ft	m
1	1a, 1b	5:00	11.7	18.8	545	166	564	17
2	2a, 2b	4:15	8.3	13.3	1312	400	1440	43
3	3a, 3b, 3c, 3d	3:30	7.9	12.7	889	271	860	26
4	4	4:00	7.3	11.8	653	199	666	20
5	5a, 5b	3:00	6.7	10.7	587	179	604	18
6	6a	3:00	6.2	9.9	942	287	164	5
7	6b, 6c, 6d	2:30	5.8	9.3	702	214	784	23
8	7a, 7b	4:00	9.0	14.5	899	274	1063	32
9	8a, 8b	4:15	9.4	15.2	876	267	653	19
10	9	4:30	8.9	14.3	1221	372	2001	6
11	10a, 10b	7:30	15.4	24.7	2041	622	2041	6

10 Days (S-N)

Our standard schedule which is popular with many walkers because the nightly s▮ are at some of the loveliest places on the WHW (usually with a pub or two and a va▮ of places to stay). It is a well-balanced route but the pace may be too slow for fit hi▮ Day 10 is long and tough: there is no accommodation mid-section to break it up.

Day	Stages	Time (hr)	Distance miles	Distance km	Ascent ft	Ascent m	Descer ft	r
1	1a, 1b	5:00	11.7	18.8	545	166	564	1
2	2a, 2b	4:15	8.3	13.3	1312	400	1440	4
3	3a, 3b, 3c, 3d	3:30	7.9	12.7	889	271	860	2
4	4	4:00	7.3	11.8	653	199	666	2
5	5a, 5b	3:00	6.7	10.7	587	179	604	1
6	6a, 6b, 6c, 6d	5:30	11.9	19.2	1644	501	948	2
7	7a, 7b	4:00	9.0	14.5	899	274	1063	3
8	8a, 8b	4:15	9.4	15.2	876	267	653	1
9	9	4:30	8.9	14.3	1221	372	2001	6
10	10a, 10b	7:30	15.4	24.7	2041	622	2041	6

Days (S-N)

e middle four days of the 10-Day itinerary are squeezed into three longer days. A
w nightly stops are at less obvious locations but that is no bad thing. You will not stay
the busy Inversnaid Hotel, opting instead for an overnight at Ardlui, accessed by a
ely ferry ride across Loch Lomond.

Day	Stages	Time (hr)	Distance		Ascent		Descent	
			miles	km	ft	m	ft	m
1	1a, 1b	5:00	11.7	18.8	545	166	564	172
2	2a, 2b	4:15	8.3	13.3	1312	400	1440	439
3	3a, 3b, 3c, 3d	3:30	7.9	12.7	889	271	860	262
4	4, 5a	5:45	11.8	19.0	883	269	866	264
5	5b, 6a, 6b, 6c	5:45	11.9	19.2	1805	550	1306	398
6	6d, 7a, 7b	5:00	11.2	18.0	1096	334	1109	338
7	8a, 8b	4:15	9.4	15.2	876	267	653	199
8	9	4:30	8.9	14.3	1221	372	2001	610
9	10a, 10b	7:30	15.4	24.7	2041	622	2041	622

Days (S-N)

s 2, 3 and 4 are long, making the first half of the trek more challenging. Days 6 and
e comparatively shorter.

Day	Stages	Time (hr)	Distance		Ascent		Descent	
			miles	km	ft	m	ft	m
1	1a, 1b	5:00	11.7	18.8	545	166	564	172
2	2a, 2b, 3a, 3b	5:30	11.6	18.6	1581	482	1690	515
3	3c, 3d, 4	6:15	11.9	19.2	1273	388	1276	389
4	5a, 5b, 6a,	6:00	12.8	20.6	1529	466	768	234
5	6b, 6c, 6d, 7a	5:15	12.3	19.8	1066	325	1348	411
6	7b, 8a	5:00	10.6	17.1	1378	420	899	274
7	8b, 9	5:00	10.2	16.4	1253	382	2254	687
8	10a, 10b	7:30	15.4	24.7	2041	622	2041	622

re are fabulous views of
 Lomond on Stage 5a

7 Days (S-N)

Days 2, 3, 4, 5 and 7 are long. Days 5 and 7 are particularly challenging but fortunate day 6 is the shortest one giving some brief respite before the arduous final day.

Day	Stages	Time (hr)	Distance		Ascent		Descent	
			miles	km	ft	m	ft	m
1	1a, 1b, 2a	5:15	12.2	19.6	604	184	564	17
2	2b, 3a, 3b, 3c	6:00	13.0	20.9	1686	514	1883	57
3	3d, 4, 5a	7:15	14.5	23.3	1339	408	1283	39
4	5b, 6a, 6b, 6c, 6d	6:45	14.1	22.7	2001	610	1352	41
5	7a, 7b, 8a	7:45	17.2	27.6	1742	531	1463	44
6	8b, 9	5:00	10.2	16.4	1253	382	2254	68
7	10a, 10b	7:30	15.4	24.7	2041	622	2041	62

6 Days (S-N)

For fit hikers. After a warm-up on day 1, every day is long and challenging. Days 4 5 are extremely tough.

Day	Stages	Time (hr)	Distance		Ascent		Descen	
			miles	km	ft	m	ft	m
1	1a, 1b, 2a	5:15	12.2	19.6	604	184	564	17
2	2b, 3a, 3b, 3c	6:00	13.0	20.9	1686	514	1883	57
3	3d, 4, 5a, 5b	8:30	16.7	26.8	1696	517	1686	51
4	6a, 6b, 6c, 6d, 7a, 7b	9:30	20.9	33.7	2543	775	2011	61
5	8a, 8b, 9	8:45	18.3	29.5	2097	639	2654	80
6	10a, 10b	7:30	15.4	24.7	2041	622	2041	62

The WHW is extremely well marked (Stage 6c)

Days (S-N)

...ough itinerary for fit and experienced walkers and runners. Every day is long and
...'d so you will need to arrive at the start in good shape. The times are based on
...king speeds (to enable accurate comparison with the other itineraries) so runners
... need to adjust them accordingly.

Day	Stages	Time (hr)	Distance		Ascent		Descent	
			miles	km	ft	m	ft	m
1	1a, 1b, 2a, 2b	9:15	20.0	32.1	1857	566	2005	611
2	3a, 3b, 3c, 3d, 4, 5a, 5b	10:30	21.9	35.2	2129	649	2129	649
3	6a, 6b, 6c, 6d, 7a, 7b	9:30	20.9	33.7	2543	775	2011	613
4	8a, 8b, 9	8:45	18.3	29.5	2097	639	2654	809
5	10a, 10b	7:30	15.4	24.7	2041	622	2041	622

Days (S-N)

...ery demanding itinerary for experienced long-distance runners. Every day is
...remely hard so you will need to arrive at the start in excellent shape. The times are
...ed on walking speeds (to enable accurate comparison with the other itineraries) so
...ners will need to adjust them accordingly.

Day	Stages	Time (hr)	Distance		Ascent		Descent	
			miles	km	ft	m	ft	m
1	1a, 1b, 2a, 2b	9:15	20.0	32.1	1857	566	2005	611
2	3a, 3b, 3c, 3d, 4, 5a, 5b, 6a	13:30	28.0	45.1	3071	936	2293	699
3	6b, 6c, 6d, 7a, 7b, 8a, 8b	10:45	24.2	39.0	2477	755	2500	762
4	9, 10a, 10b	12:00	24.2	39.0	3261	994	4042	1232

Days (S-N)

...ery demanding itinerary for experienced long-distance runners. Every day is
...ally long with huge altitude gain and loss. The times are based on walking speeds
...enable accurate comparison with the other itineraries) so runners will need to
...st them accordingly.

Day	Stages	Time (hr)	Distance		Ascent		Descent	
			miles	km	ft	m	ft	m
1	1a, 1b, 2a, 2b, 3a, 3b, 3c, 3d	12:45	27.8	44.8	2746	837	2864	873
2	4, 5a, 5b, 6a, 6b, 6c, 6d, 7a, 7b	16:30	34.9	56.2	3783	1153	3281	1000
3	8a, 8b, 9, 10a, 10b	16:15	33.7	54.2	4137	1261	4695	1431

Suggested Itineraries: North to South

10 Days (N-S)

Our standard schedule which is popular with many walkers because the nightly st... are at some of the loveliest places on the WHW (usually with a pub or two and a vari... of places to stay). Unfortunately, the first stage is the hardest which is why most peo... prefer to hike S-N. After the first day, it is a reasonably well-balanced itinerary but ... pace may be too slow for fit hikers.

Day	Stages	Time (hr)	Distance miles	km	Ascent ft	m	Descent ft	m
1	10b, 10a	7:30	15.4	24.7	2041	622	2041	62
2	9	5:00	8.9	14.3	2001	610	1221	37
3	8b, 8a	4:15	9.4	15.2	653	199	876	26
4	7b, 7a	4:15	9.0	14.5	1063	324	899	2:
5	6d, 6c, 6b, 6a	5:15	11.9	19.2	948	289	1644	5(
6	5b, 5a	3:00	6.7	10.7	604	184	587	1
7	4	4:00	7.3	11.8	666	203	653	1(
8	3d, 3c, 3b, 3a	3:30	7.9	12.7	860	262	889	2:
9	2b, 2a	4:15	8.3	13.3	1440	439	1312	4
10	1b, 1a	5:00	11.7	18.8	564	172	545	1

9 Days (N-S)

The middle four days of the 10-Day itinerary are squeezed into three longer day... few nightly stops are at less obvious locations but that is no bad thing. You will not... at the busy Inversnaid Hotel, opting instead for an overnight at Ardlui, accessed... lovely ferry ride across Loch Lomond. The first stage is the hardest.

Day	Stages	Time (hr)	Distance miles	km	Ascent ft	m	Descent ft	m
1	10b, 10a	7:30	15.4	24.7	2041	622	2041	6:
2	9	5:00	8.9	14.3	2001	610	1221	3
3	8b, 8a	4:15	9.4	15.2	653	199	876	2(
4	7b, 7a, 6d	5:15	11.2	18.0	1109	338	1096	3
5	6c, 6b, 6a, 5b	5:30	11.9	19.2	1306	398	1805	5
6	5a, 4	5:45	11.8	19.0	866	264	883	2
7	3d, 3c, 3b, 3a	3:30	7.9	12.7	860	262	889	2
8	2b, 2a	4:15	8.3	13.3	1440	439	1312	4
9	1b, 1a	5:00	11.7	18.8	564	172	545	1

Days (N-S)

ere is plenty of climbing on Days 1 and 2 making for a tough introduction to the trek.
fact, like the 9 and 10 Day itineraries, day 1 is the hardest stage of all.

Day	Stages	Time (hr)	Distance		Ascent		Descent	
			miles	km	ft	m	ft	m
1	10b, 10a	7:30	15.4	24.7	2041	622	2041	622
2	9, 8b	5:45	10.2	16.4	2254	687	1253	382
3	8a, 7b	4:45	10.6	17.1	899	274	1378	420
4	7a, 6d, 6c, 6b	5:45	12.3	19.8	1348	411	1066	325
5	6a, 5b, 5a	5:30	12.8	20.6	768	234	1529	466
6	4, 3d, 3c	6:15	11.9	19.2	1276	389	1273	388
7	3b, 3a, 2b	5:15	11.1	17.8	1690	515	1522	464
8	2a, 1b, 1a	5:15	12.2	19.6	564	172	604	184

Days (N-S)

 first day is one of the hardest so you will want to be in good shape before you start.
s 3, 4, 5 and 6 are also long. The final day is the easiest.

Day	Stages	Time (hr)	Distance		Ascent		Descent	
			miles	km	ft	m	ft	m
1	10b, 10a	7:30	15.4	24.7	2041	622	2041	622
2	9, 8b	5:45	10.2	16.4	2254	687	1253	382
3	8a, 7b, 7a	7:45	17.2	27.6	1463	446	1742	531
4	6d, 6c, 6b, 6a, 5b	6:30	14.1	22.7	1352	412	2001	610
5	5a, 4, 3d	7:15	14.5	23.3	1283	391	1339	408
6	3c, 3b, 3a, 2b	6:00	13.0	20.9	1883	574	1686	514
7	2a, 1b, 1a	5:15	12.2	19.6	564	172	604	184

Days (N-S)

fit hikers. It starts hard and remains hard until the final day which is much more
king. Days 2 and 3 are particularly tough.

Day	Stages	Time (hr)	Distance		Ascent		Descent	
			miles	km	ft	m	ft	m
1	10b, 10a	7:30	15.4	24.7	2041	622	2041	622
2	9, 8b, 8a	9:15	18.3	29.5	2654	809	2097	639
3	7b, 7a, 6d, 6c, 6b, 6a	9:30	20.9	33.7	2011	613	2543	775
	5b, 5a, 4, 3d	8:30	16.7	26.8	1686	514	1696	517
	3c, 3b, 3a, 2b	6:00	13.0	20.9	1883	574	1686	514
	2a, 1b, 1a	5:15	12.2	19.6	564	172	604	184

5 Days (N-S)

A tough itinerary for fit and experienced walkers and runners. Every day is long a hard so you will need to arrive at the start in good shape. The times are based walking speeds (to enable accurate comparison with the other itineraries) so runn will need to adjust them accordingly.

Day	Stages	Time (hr)	Distance		Ascent		Descent	
			miles	km	ft	m	ft	m
1	10b, 10a	7:30	15.4	24.7	2041	622	2041	62:
2	9, 8b, 8a	9:15	18.3	29.5	2654	809	2097	63'
3	7b, 7a, 6d, 6c, 6b, 6a	9:30	20.9	33.7	2011	613	2543	77.
4	5b, 5a, 4, 3d, 3c, 3b, 3a	10:30	21.9	35.2	2129	649	2129	64
5	2b, 2a, 1b, 1a	9:15	20.0	32.1	2005	611	1857	56

4 Days (N-S)

A very demanding itinerary for experienced long-distance runners. Every day extremely hard so you will need to arrive at the start in excellent shape. The times based on walking speeds (to enable accurate comparison with the other itineraries runners will need to adjust them accordingly.

Day	Stages	Time (hr)	Distance		Ascent		Descen	
			miles	km	ft	m	ft	n
1	10b, 10a, 9	12:30	24.2	39.0	4042	1232	3261	9!
2	8b, 8a, 7b, 7a, 6d, 6c, 6b	11:15	24.2	39.0	2500	762	2477	7:
3	6a, 5b, 5a, 4, 3d, 3c, 3b, 3a	13:00	28.0	45.1	2293	699	3071	9:
4	2b, 2a, 1b, 1a	9:15	20.0	32.1	2005	611	1857	5(

3 Days (N-S)

A very demanding itinerary for experienced long-distance runners. Every da brutally long with huge altitude gain and loss. The times are based on walking sp (to enable accurate comparison with the other itineraries) so runners will nee adjust them accordingly.

Day	Stages	Time (hr)	Distance		Ascent		Descer	
			miles	km	ft	m	ft	r
1	10b, 10a, 9, 8b	13.25	25.54	41.1	4295	1309	3294	1(
2	8a, 7b, 7a, 6d, 6c, 6b, 6a, 5b, 5a	16.00	35.74	57.5	3015	919	3973	1:
3	4, 3d, 3c, 3b, 3a, 2b, 2a, 1b, 1a	16.75	35.18	56.6	3530	1076	3399	1(

accommodation

famous statue in Fort William

WHW is a popular trek and there is a wide range of accommodation: 'bed and [brea]kfasts', pubs, hotels, hostels, bunkhouses/camping barns and a few bothies. All [acco]mmodation is numbered and marked on the OS maps in this book. Detailed [acco]mmodation listings are provided on pages 24 to 32. All contact details were correct [at th]e date of press but be aware that this information frequently changes. Please let us [kno]w about any changes you notice. For camping, see page 21.

[Alth]ough there is plenty of accommodation along the trail itself, it tends to book up very [quic]kly. As you move further away from the trail, bookings are often easier to secure. In [the]accommodation listings, off-route accommodation is labelled 'OR' and we indicate [exac]tly how far from the trail it is located. Bear in mind that the extra time and distance [requ]ired to travel to, and from, OR accommodation is excluded from the statistics for each [stag]e in the Itinerary Planner: if you intend to stay OR, you will need to allow for this extra [time] and effort when planning.

[Thes]e days, most people have their entire trip booked before they depart. The rise in the [num]ber of companies offering unguided trips means that an increasing number of WHW [beds] are block-booked months in advance. This makes it harder for the independent [trek]ker to stay at some of the best locations unless you book well in advance or you are [prep]ared to camp.

[In Ju]ly/August and during public holidays, the trail is very busy and forward booking is [virtu]ally essential. You might get lucky and be able to cobble together a set of bookings [at th]e last minute but you are unlikely to get 'first-choice' accommodation right next to [the t]rail.

[Even] outside of July/August, it is wise to book ahead, particularly at weekends and on [stag]es where there is only one place to stay. That said, in April, May, June, September [and O]ctober, it is still perfectly possible for the independent trekker to secure last-minute [book]ings, particularly if you are flexible with dates and places and are prepared to stay in [town]s/villages a short distance OR. Some OR places may be willing to pick you up from [the t]rail and leave you back the next morning: check when booking. Alternatively, there [are lo]cal taxi companies which will pick you up: see 'Public transport along the WHW'.

[In Ap]ril (excluding Easter) and October, fewer people walk the route so there is less demand [for ac]commodation. Before April, and from November onwards, some accommodation [may]be closed so check in advance. For more booking tips, see page 33.

Bed & Breakfasts (B&Bs):

these form the back-bone of WH accommodation. Traditionally, they were private homes which offered rooms a breakfast to visitors. Nowadays, however, you find many bigger and more profession run properties. Bed and breakfast normally cost £35-70 per person sharing a double/tw room. Rates for solo travellers are usually higher because they pay a single occupanc rate. Normally, the ensuite bedrooms are basic but clean and comfortable. 'Full Scott breakfast is the norm: a large helping of bacon, sausage, eggs, mushrooms and bl pudding. Most do not provide evening meals but the owner should be able to recommen a local pub or restaurant. Most B&Bs have their own websites and many list their rooms the generic travel booking sites such as expedia.com or booking.com.

Pubs & Inns:

most villages have a pub and many of them offer bed and break accommodation. This normally costs £35-70 per person sharing a double/twin roo Rates for solo travellers are usually higher because they pay a single occupancy r Evening meals are usually available and the standard of food these days is fairly h Many of the pubs serve a selection of local craft beers: for some, this is a highlight of WHW. Most pubs have their own websites.

Hotels:

the hotels on offer range from basic ones to more luxury properties. Pr vary widely. They all provide 'Full Scottish' breakfasts and most also offer evening me Most hotels have their own websites and many list their rooms on the generic tr booking sites such as expedia.com or booking.com.

Hostels:

these offer beds in dormitories and sometimes private rooms. Gener they will have shared bathrooms, self-catering kitchen facilities and communal a Continental breakfast (tea and toast) is sometimes available. Bedding is usually supp Like B&Bs, hostels are becoming more upmarket and prices rise along with the quali the offering. A bed usually costs £20-30 per person. Groups of two or more may find E to be better value.

Bunkhouses & camping barns:

these provide beds in dormito Quality varies and often the accommodation is very basic: you will usually need to b your own sleeping bag. Sometimes there will be showers and self-catering facilities. P are low.

Bothies:

these are basic shelters which are left unlocked and are available for any to use. There are two on the WHW: Rowchoish Bothy (Stage 4; see images below) Doune Byre Bothy (Stage 5a). They are unique to GB and are run by the Mountain Bo Association (www.mountainbothies.org.uk). Sometimes they have a sleeping plat but often you will sleep on the floor. There are no mattresses: you bring your own slee bag and mat. They do not have toilet facilities: a spade is provided! They are free of ch to use but it is first come, first served. Users should respect the 'Bothy Code' whi usually displayed at the bothies.

Rowchoish Bothy (Stage 4)

amping

The wild camping area at Inveroran (Stage 7b/8a)

ping is the cheapest way to hike the WHW: wild camping (see below) is free of charge
is permitted along much of the WHW, and a pitch at a commercial site costs only
5 per person per night. Camping also offers more freedom because you can usually
st your itinerary as you go: campsites rarely need to be booked far in advance (except
ng July/August and public holiday weekends) and wild camping requires no booking
(except in LLTNP permit areas). There are many commercial campsites along the trail
normally, they are clean and well-maintained: they can be some of the loveliest places
he WHW to spend the night. Showers are available but occasionally, you may pay
le extra for this luxury. Even if you have booked in advance, it is always sensible to
phone at least a day or two before so the campsite knows when to expect you.

elp campers plan, we have set out below a list of commercial sites and specifically
ated wild camping spots: however, there are countless other opportunities for
campers. Contact details and information on the facilities are set out in the full
mmodation Listings (see pages 24 to 32). Wild camping spots (specifically allocated
herwise) have no facilities.

obvious downside to camping is that you need to carry a lot more gear: tents,
ing mats, sleeping bags and stoves all add weight to your pack, making the trek
difficult. In the 'Equipment' section, we provide advice on how to lighten your load.
ever, another solution is to use a baggage transfer service to transfer your heavy bags
een campsites (see 'Baggage transfer').

ld camping

cottish Outdoor Access Code (SOAC) gives hikers rights to access most land provided
hey behave responsibly. These rights extend to wild camping and consequently, a
many people wild camp on the WHW. The SOAC allows wild camping on hills and
s, in forests and woods, on beaches, beside rivers and lochs, in parks and on some
of farmland. You should not camp in fields containing crops or animals and you
d keep well away from buildings, roads and historic structures. You should leave
ace and be sure to follow the provisions of the SOAC (particularly the guidance for
ng fires): see **www.outdooraccess-scotland.scot** for further information. Also see
ild Camping Guidelines below.

21

Although the SOAC permits wild camping along much of the WHW, the situation different in the LLTNP: local bye-laws have introduced 'Camping Management Zon (CMZs) within the park. Outside these CMZs, wild camping is permitted as normal, inside them wild camping is generally prohibited between 1 March and 30 Septem For WHW trekkers, this means that, for most of the trekking season, wild campin prohibited in the following areas:

▶ along Loch Lomond between Balmaha (Stage 2b/3a) and Ptarmigan Lodge (N Rowardennan; Stage 4); and

▶ Glen Falloch, a short distance either side of Inverarnan (on Stages 5b and 6a)

Fortunately, within the CMZs, there are some commercial campsites. More confusir however, there are also designated 'permit areas' within the CMZs where you can camp with a permit: you can camp anywhere within the permit areas but there are formal facilities. There are a limited number of permits each night: book in advanc **www.lochlomond-trossachs.org**. There is only one such permit area that is of us WHW trekkers: it is near Lochan Maoil Dhuinne on Stage 3d (before Rowardennan).

Wild camping guidelines

The number of wild campers in GB has increased greatly in recent years. It is there more important than ever to respect the land and the landowners' wishes. WHW trek who plan to camp wild should respect the provisions of the SOAC and comply with following important rules:

▶ **Leave no trace:** you should leave the environment in exactly the same conditic you found it. Leave nothing behind and take nothing away with you. When you packed up and are ready to leave, look back on your campsite and make sure another person would not be able to tell that you have been there (except fo flattened grass where your tent was pitched).

▶ **Avoid lighting an open fire:** climate change is upon us and bush-fires are becom more common in GB. Much of the WHW is close to wooded areas and moorlan open fires during dry weather carry risk. Do not be that person who accider destroys acres of pristine countryside.

▶ **Perform toilet duties responsibly:** this means that you should use a trowel to hole in which to 'do your business'. There are some incredibly lightweight backpac trowels available these days. Your hole should be at least 30m from water-course the hole in afterwards and carry away your used toilet paper in a bag that you brought along specifically for that purpose. Defecating and placing a stone on t not acceptable: animals can move stones and imagine how you would feel if yo down next to such a place! Also carry out tampons and sanitary towels.

▶ **Be discreet and have respect for others:** try to camp where others cannot see Keep your group small: it is supposed to be a 'wild' experience. Do not make a noise at night.

▶ **Stay for only one night** at a particular spot and then move on.

Stage		Campsite
1a (0.5-1 mile OR)	**4** 🏠	West Highland Way Campsite
1a/1b	**8** 🏠	Drymen Camping
3a/3b	**32** 🏠	Milarrochy Bay Camping & Caravanning Club Site
3b/3c	**33** 🏠	Cashel Campsite
3c/3d	**35** 🏠	Sallochy Campsite
3d	N/A	LLTNP permit area
4/5a Inversnaid (0.8 miles OR)	**42** 🏠	Inversnaid Bunkhouse
5a	N/A	Specifically allocated wild camping area (a few minutes N of Inversnaid Hotel)
5a/5b Ardlui (OR)	**45** 🏠	Ardlui Holiday Park
5b/6a Inverarnan	**46** 🏠	Beinglas Farm Campsite
6c/6d	**58** 🏠	Strathfillan Wigwam Village
6d/7a Tyndrum	**60** 🏠	Pine Trees Camping Park
6d/7a Tyndrum	**61** 🏠	By the Way Hostel & Campsite
7a/7b Bridge of Orchy	N/A	Specifically allocated wild camping area (a few minutes W of Bridge of Orchy Hotel)
7b/8a Inveroran	N/A	Specifically allocated wild camping area (a few minutes W of Inveroran Hotel)
8a/8b	**73** 🏠	Glencoe Mountain Resort
9/10a Kinlochleven	**75** 🏠	Blackwater Hostel & Campsite
9/10a Kinlochleven	**84** 🏠	MacDonald Hotel & Cabins
10a/10b Glen Nevis	**89** 🏠	Glen Nevis Caravan & Camping Park

Accommodation Listings

Legend:
- 🛏 Dormitory/Bunkhouse
- 🔒🍽 Private Room
- ⛺ Camping
- 🍷 Drinks
- 🍔 Lunch
- 🍴 Evening Meals
- 🥐 Breakfast
- 🛒 Food shop
- 📶 WiFi
- **OR** Off-route

Stage		Name	Facilities	Contact Details
1a Milngavie	**1**	Premier Inn Glasgow Milngavie	🔒🍽 📶 🍷 🥐 🍔 🍴	0333 777 7286 www.premierinn.com
1a Milngavie	**2**	Premier Inn Glasgow Bearsden	🔒🍽 📶 🍷 🥐 🍔 🍴	0333 777 7282 www.premierinn.com
1a (0.6 miles OR)	**3**	Ardoch House	🔒🍽 📶 🥐 🍴	07488 261 730
1a (0.5-1 mile OR)	**4**	West Highland Way Campsite	⛺ 📶 🍷 🥐 🍔 🍴 long-term parking	07488 261 730
1a Strathblane (2.6 miles OR)	**5**	Kirkhouse Inn	🔒🍽 📶 🍷 🥐 🍔 🍴	01360 771 771 info@kirkhouseinn.com www.kirkhouseinn.com
1a (2.1 miles OR)	**6**	The Attic	🔒🍽 🛏 📶 🍷 🥐 🍔 🍴	01360 770 500 info@theattic.scot www.theattic.scot
1a Croftamie (1.8 miles OR)	**7**	Croftburn B&B	🔒🍽 📶 🥐	01360 660 796 hello@croftburn.co.uk www.croftburn.co.uk
1a/1b	**8**	Drymen Camping	⛺ 🔒🍽 📶	07494 144 064 www.drymencamping.co.uk

Stage		Name	Facilities	Contact Details
1a/1b	**9** 🏠	Altquhur Byre B&B	🔒 ☕ Take-away pizza available	07980 889 790 altquhurbyre@gmail.com www.altquhurbyre.co.uk
1a	**10** 🏠	Duncan Family Farms Glamping Pods	🔒 📶 Ready meals available	07749 931 144/01360 660 609 shona@duncanfamilyfarms.co.uk www.duncanfamilyfarms.co.uk
1b/2a	**11** 🏠	Mulberry Lodge	🔒 📶 ☕	01360 660094 info@mulberrylodge.co.uk www.mulberrylodge.co.uk
1b/2a Drymen 5 miles OR)	**12** 🏠	Buchanan Arms Hotel	🔒 📶 🍷 ☕ 🍔 🍴	01360 660 588 info@buchananarms.co.uk www.buchananarms.co.uk
1b/2a Drymen 5 miles OR)	**13** 🏠	The Winnock Hotel	🔒 📶 🍷 ☕ 🍔 🍴	01360 660 245 info@winnockhotel.com www.winnockhotel.com
1b/2a Drymen 5 miles OR)	**14** 🏠	The Clachan Inn	🔒 📶 🍷 ☕ 🍔 🍴	01360 660 824 info@clachaninndrymen.co.uk www.clachaninndrymen.co.uk
1b/2a Drymen 5 miles OR)	**15** 🏠	The Drymen Inn	🔒 📶 🍷 ☕ 🍔 🍴	01360 660 321 info@thedrymeninn.com www.thedrymeninn.com
1b/2a Drymen 5 miles OR)	**16** 🏠	Braeside Guest House	🔒 📶	01360 660 989 braesidelochlomond@gmail.com www.braeside-drymen.co.uk
1b/2a Drymen miles OR)	**17** 🏠	The Hawthorns B&B	🔒 📶 ☕	07878 360 258 alan@hawthorns-drymen.com www.hawthorns-drymen.com
1b/2a Drymen miles OR)	**18** 🏠	Elmbank B&B	🔒 📶 ☕	01360 661 016 enquiries@elmbank-drymen.co.uk www.elmbank-drymen.com
1b/2a Drymen miles OR)	**19** 🏠	Ashbank B&B	🔒 📶 ☕	01360 660 049 info@ashbank-drymen.co.uk www.ashbank-drymen.co.uk
1b/2a Drymen miles OR)	**20** 🏠	Bolzicco's B&B	🔒 📶 ☕	07837 718 011 bolziccosdrymen@gmail.com www.bolziccos.com
1b/2a Drymen miles OR)	**21** 🏠	Lander B&B	🔒 📶 ☕	01360 660 273 www.bandb.labbs.com
1b/2a Drymen miles OR)	**22** 🏠	Glenlaird B&B	🔒 📶 ☕	01360 661026 contact@glenlaird.co.uk www.glenlaird.co.uk

Stage		Name	Facilities	Contact Details
1b/2a Drymen (0.5 miles OR)	23	Kip in the Kirk	🔒📶🛏📶☕	07734 394 315 www.kipinthekirk.co.uk
1b/2a Drymen (2 miles OR)	24	Green Shadows B&B	🔒📶☕ Free pick up from Drymen	07775 690 855/01360 660 289 greenshadows@hotmail.com www.greenshadowsbandb.com
2a/2b	25	Glenalva B&B	🔒📶☕	01360 660 491 www.glenalva-bed-and-breakfast.business.site
2b/3a Balmaha	26	Oak Tree Inn	🔒📶🍷☕🍔🍴	01360 870 357 info@theoaktreeinn.co.uk www.theoaktreeinn.co.uk
2b/3a Balmaha	27	Bay Cottage B&B	🔒📶☕	01360 870 346 lizbates55@hotmail.com www.lochlomond-baycottage.co.u
2b/3a Balmaha	28	Balmaha Lodges	🔒📶	01360 870 052 bookings@balmahalodges.com www.balmahalodges.com
2b/3a Balmaha	29	Balmaha House B&B/ Balmaha Bunkhouse	🔒📶🛏📶☕	01360 870 006 www.balmahahouse.com
2b/3a Balmaha	30	Arrochoile B&B	🔒📶☕	01360 870 231 bb.arrochoile@gmail.com www.whw-bb-lochlomond.com
2b/3a Balmaha	31	Birchwood Guest Lodge	🔒	www.birchwoodguestlodge.co.uk
3a/3b	32	Milarrochy Bay Camping & Caravanning Club Site	⛺📶	024 7647 5426 www.campingandcaravanningclu co.uk
3b/3c	33	Cashel Campsite	⛺	024 7642 3008 www.campingintheforest.co.uk
3c (0.2 miles OR)	34	The Shepherd's House B&B	🔒☕	www.theshepherdshouse.co.uk
3c/3d	35	Sallochy Campsite	⛺	07826 935 016 sallochy.wardens@forestryandlar gov.scot www.forestryandland.gov.scot
3d/4 Rowardennan	36	Rowardennan Hotel	🔒📶🍷☕🍔🍴	01360 870 273 overnight@rowardennanhotel.cc www.rowardennanhotel.co.uk

Stage		Name	Facilities	Contact Details
3d/4 owardennan	**37**	The Lodge at Loch Lomond	Groceries available for delivery	07500 057 882 kkmpropertiesltd@gmail.com www.lodgeatlochlomond.com
4 owardennan	**38**	Rowardennan Lodge Youth Hostel		01360 870 259 rowardennan@hostellingscotland.org.uk www.hostellingscotland.org.uk
4 owardennan	**39**	Ben Lomond Bunkhouse		07837 784 120/01360 870 224 benlomond@nts.org.uk www.nts.org.uk
4	**40**	Rowchoish Bothy	N/A	www.mountainbothies.org.uk
4/5a Inversnaid	**41**	Inversnaid Hotel		01877 386 223 inversnaidhotel@lochsandglens.com www.inversnaidhotel.com
4/5a Inversnaid .8 miles OR)	**42**	Inversnaid Bunkhouse		The business was for sale at date of press so its future is uncertain 01877 386249 hostel@inversnaid.com www.inversnaid.com
4/5a nversnaid 1 miles OR)	**43**	Garrison of Inversnaid B&B		01877 386 341 enquiries@garrisonofinversnaid.co.uk www.garrisonofinversnaid.co.uk
5a	**44**	Doune Byre Bothy	N/A	www.mountainbothies.org.uk
5a/5b Ardlui (OR)	**45**	Ardlui Holiday Park		01301 704 243 info@ardlui.co.uk www.ardlui.com
5b/6a verarnan	**46**	Beinglas Farm Campsite		01301 704 281 www.beinglascampsite.co.uk
5b/6a verarnan	**47**	The Drovers' Inn		01301 704 234 info@thedroversinn.co.uk www.droversinn.co.uk
5b/6a verarnan	**48**	Rose Cottage B&B		01301 704 255

Stage		Name	Facilities	Contact Details
6a/6b Crianlarich (1 mile OR)	49	Best Western The Crianlarich Hotel	🅿 📶 🍷 ☕ 🍔 🍴	01838 300 272 info@crianlarich-hotel.co.uk www.crianlarich-hotel.co.uk
6a/6b Crianlarich (1 mile OR)	50	Glenbruar House	🅿 📶 ☕	01838 300268 www.glenbruar-crianlarich-bandb.co.uk
6a/6b Crianlarich (1 mile OR)	51	Hillview B&B	🅿 📶 ☕	01838 300 323 anngillies@btinternet.com www.crianlarichbandb.co.uk
6a/6b Crianlarich (1 mile OR)	52	Craigbank Guest House	🅿 📶 ☕	01838 300 279 stay@craigbankguesthouse.com www.craigbankguesthouse.com
6a/6b Crianlarich (1 mile OR)	53	Glenardran Guest House	🅿 📶 ☕	01838 300 236/07387 170 711 mail@glenardran.co.uk www.glenardran.co.uk
6a/6b Crianlarich (1 mile OR)	54	Ben More Lodge	🅿 📶 🍷 ☕ 🍔 🍴	01838 300 210 info@ben-more.co.uk www.ben-more.co.uk
6a/6b Crianlarich (1 mile OR)	55	Crianlarich Youth Hostel	🅿 🛏 📶 ☕ 🍷 🛒	01838 300 260 crianlarich@hostellingscotland.org.uk www.hostellingscotland.org.uk
6a/6b Crianlarich (1 mile OR)	56	Inverardran B&B	🅿 📶 ☕	01838 300 240/07979 690 004 inverardran@gmail.com www.inverardran.co.uk
6b/6c (0.3 miles OR)	57	Ewich House B&B	🅿 📶 ☕	01838 300 536/07484 870 159 enquiries@ewich.co.uk www.ewich.co.uk
6c/6d	58	Strathfillan Wigwam Village	🅿 ⛺ 📶 🛒	www.wigwamholidays.com
6d/7a Tyndrum	59	Glengarry House	🅿 📶 ☕	01838 400 224 enquiries@glengarryhouse.com www.glengarryhouse.com
6d/7a Tyndrum	60	Pine Trees Camping Park	🅿 ⛺ 📶 🛒	01838 400 349 enquiries@pinetreescaravanpark.co.uk www.pinetreescaravanpark.co.uk
6d/7a Tyndrum	61	By the Way Hostel & Campsite	🅿 🛏 ⛺ 📶	01838 400 333 info@tyndrumbytheway.com www.tyndrumbytheway.com
6d/7a Tyndrum	62	Tigh-na-Fraoch B&B	🅿 📶 ☕	01838 400 354 info@tigh-na-fraoch.com www.tigh-na-fraoch.com

Stage		Name	Facilities	Contact Details
6d/7a Tyndrum	**63**	Tyndrum Lodges	🔒 📶	07793 037 425 info@tyndrumlodges.co.uk www.tyndrumlodges.co.uk
6d/7a Tyndrum	**64**	Muthu Ben Doran Hotel	🔒 📶 🍷 ☕ 🍔 🍴	01838 400 373 mbd.reception@muthuhotels.com www.muthuhotelsmgm.com
6d/7a Tyndrum	**65**	Dalkell Cottage Guest House	🔒 📶 ☕	01838 400 285 info@dalkell.com www.dalkell.com
6d/7a Tyndrum	**66**	The Tyndrum Inn	🔒 📶 🍷 ☕ 🍔 🍴	01838 400 219 info@thetyndruminn.co.uk www.thetyndruminn.co.uk
6d/7a Tyndrum	**67**	Clifton Cottage B&B	🔒 📶 ☕	01838 400 533 www.cliftoncottage.business.site
7a/7b Bridge of Orchy	**68**	West Highland Way Sleeper	🛏 ☕ 🍔 🍴	07778 746 600 thewesthighlandwaysleeper@gmail.com www.westhighlandwaysleeper.com
7a/7b Bridge of Orchy	**69**	Taransay Cottage B&B	🔒 📶 ☕	07943 215 677 stay@taransaycottage.com www.taransaycottage.com
7a/7b Bridge of Orchy	**70**	Bridge of Orchy Hotel	🔒 📶 🍷 ☕ 🍔 🍴	01838 400 208 info@bridgeoforchy.co.uk www.bridgeoforchy.co.uk
7a/7b Bridge of Orchy	**71**	Stance Cottage B&B	🔒 ☕	07500 904 502 stancecottagebandb@gmail.com www.stancecottagebandb.com
7b/8a Inveroran	**72**	Inveroran Hotel	🔒 📶 🍷 ☕ 🍔 🍴	01838 400 250 booking@inveroran.com www.inveroran.com
8a/8b	**73**	Glencoe Mountain Resort	🔒 ⛺ New café under construction	01855 851 226 admin@glencoemountain.co.uk www.glencoemountain.co.uk
8b/9	**74**	Kingshouse Hotel	🔒 🛏 📶 ☕ 🍔 🍴 🍷 Laundry Facilities	01855 851 259 contact@kingshousehotel.co.uk www.kingshousehotel.co.uk
9/10a Kinlochleven	**75**	Blackwater Hostel & Campsite	🔒 ⛺ 📶	01855 831 253 stay@blackwaterhostel.co.uk www.blackwaterhostel.co.uk

Stage		Name	Facilities	Contact Details
9/10a Kinlochleven	76	Forest View Guesthouse	🔒📶☕	01855 831 302 info@forestviewbnb.co.uk www.forestviewbnb.co.uk
9/10a Kinlochleven	77	West Highland Lodge	🔒📶	01855 831 253 stay@blackwaterhostel.co.uk www.blackwaterhostel.co.uk
9/10a Kinlochleven	78	Highland Getaway Inn	🔒📶🍷☕🍔🍴	01855 831 258
9/10a Kinlochleven	79	Allt-na-Leven Guest House	🔒📶☕	01855 831 366 stay@bedandbreakfastkinlochleven.co.uk www.bedandbreakfastkinlochleven.co.uk
9/10a Kinlochleven	80	Bank House B&B	🔒📶☕	07514 620 188/07587 336 127 bankhousebooking@protonmail.com www.bankhousebedandbreakfast.com
9/10a Kinlochleven	81	Tigh Na Cheo Guest House	🔒📶☕	01855 831 434 reception@tigh-na-cheo.co.uk www.tigh-na-cheo.co.uk
9/10a Kinlochleven	82	Edencoille B&B	🔒📶☕	01855 831 358 edencoille@btinternet.com www.kinlochlevenbedandbreakfast.co.uk
9/10a Kinlochleven	83	The Tailrace Inn	🔒📶🍷☕🍔🍴	01855 831 777 tailraceinn1@outlook.com www.thetailraceinn.co.uk
9/10a Kinlochleven	84	MacDonald Hotel & Cabins	🔒⛺📶☕🍔🍴🍷	01855 831 902 enquiries@macdonaldhotel.co.uk www.macdonaldhotel.co.uk
9/10a Kinlochleven	85	Failte Guest House	🔒📶☕	01855 831 394
9/10a Kinlochleven	86	Hermon B&B	🔒📶☕	01855 831 383
10a/10b Glen Nevis	87	Ben Nevis Inn	🔒📶🍷☕🍔🍴	01397 701 227 info@ben-nevis-inn.co.uk www.ben-nevis-inn.co.uk
10a/10b Glen Nevis	88	Achintee Farm	🔒📶☕	07497 082 820 bnb@achinteefarm.com www.achinteefarm.com

Stage		Name	Facilities	Contact Details
10a/10b Glen Nevis	89	Glen Nevis Caravan & Camping Park	🔒🍴 🛖 ☕ 🛏️ 🍴 🍷 🏷️ Laundry	01397 702 191 holidays@glen-nevis.co.uk www.glen-nevis.co.uk
10a/10b Glen Nevis	90	Glen Nevis Youth Hostel	🔒🍴 🛏️ 📶 ☕ 🛏️ 🍴 🍷 Laundry	01397 702 336 glennevis@hostellingscotland.org.uk www.hostellingscotland.org.uk
10b Fort William	91	Fort William Backpackers	🔒🍴 🛏️ 📶 ☕ Laundry	01397 700 711 info@fortwilliambackpackers.com www.fortwilliambackpackers.com
10b Fort William	92	Alexandra Hotel	🔒🍴 📶 🍷 ☕ 🛏️ 🍴	01397 702 241 salesalexandra@strathmorehotels.com www.strathmorehotels-thealexandra.com
10b Fort William	93	Travelodge Fort William	🔒🍴 📶 ☕	08719 846 419 www.travelodge.co.uk
10b Fort William	94	Muthu Fort William Hotel	🔒🍴 📶 🍷 ☕ 🛏️ 🍴	0845 468 0164 www.muthuhotelsmgm.com
10b Fort William	95	Cruachan Hotel	🔒🍴 📶 🍷 ☕ 🛏️ 🍴	01397 702 022 stay@cruachanhotel.co.uk www.cruachanhotel.co.uk
10b Fort William	96	Lime Tree	🔒🍴 📶 🍷 ☕ 🛏️ 🍴	01397 701 806 www.limetreefortwilliam.co.uk
10b Fort William	97	Bank Street Lodge	🔒🍴 📶	01397 700 070 www.bankstreetlodge.co.uk
10b Fort William	98	The Garrison Hotel	🔒🍴 📶 ☕	01397 602 021 stay@thegarrisonhotel.co.uk www.thegarrisonhotel.co.uk
10b Fort William	99	Ardblair B&B	🔒🍴 📶 ☕	01397 708 562 www.ardblairfortwilliam.co.uk
10b Fort William	100	Constantia House	🔒🍴 📶 ☕	01397 702 893
10b Fort William	101	St. Andrew's Guest House	🔒🍴 📶 ☕	01397 703 038
10b Fort William	102	Guisachan Guesthouse	🔒🍴 📶 ☕	01397 703 797 guisachanhouse@outlook.com www.guisachanguesthouse.co.uk

Stage		Name	Facilities	Contact Details
10b Fort William	103	Berkeley Guesthouse		01397 701 185
10b Fort William	104	Craig Nevis Guest House		01397 702 023 craignevisguesthouse.ftwm@gmail.com www.craignevis.co.uk
10b Fort William	105	Premier Inn Fort William		0333 777 7268 www.premierinn.com
10b Fort William	106	Nevis Bank Hotel		01397 705 721 stay@nevisbankinn.co.uk www.nevisbankinn.co.uk
10b Fort William	107	Distillery Guest House		info@distilleryguesthouse.com www.distilleryguesthouse.com
10b Fort William	108	Tigh Na Drochaid		01397 704 177 tighnadrochaidbb@gmail.com www.glennevisbb.co.uk
10b Fort William	109	Ben Nevis Guest House		01397 708 817 stay@bennevisguesthouse.co.uk www.bennevisguesthouse.co.uk
10b Fort William	110	The Brevins Guest House		01397 701 412/07841 388 931 info@thebrevins.co.uk www.thebrevins.co.uk

Fort William (Stage 10b)

Moody scenes on the moorland of Black Mount (Stage 8a)

ooking Tips

The WHW becomes more popular each year. To ensure that you secure your accommodation of choice, book as early as you can. Many trekkers start booking in autumn (just after the current summer season has ended) for the following season.

Try to book 'hot-spots' first: generally, these are places where there are only a few accommodation options. Once you have secured the accommodation which books up most quickly, you can normally slot in the rest of your accommodation more easily. If you leave hot-spots until last then you might have to unwind and rebook other reservations if any hot-spots that you desire are unavailable.

Start mid-week. A large number of trekkers start the trail at the weekend. Those who start mid-week are often 'out of sync' with the bulk of the trekkers and may therefore find accommodation more easily.

Weekends are normally busier (even in low season).

If you cannot get accommodation along the WHW itself, try looking for beds in towns/villages a few miles away.

Those who hike alone, or in pairs, will find it easiest to find beds. For larger groups, it is more difficult.

If you cannot secure the accommodation that you need then contact one of the unguided tour companies or accommodation booking services. They block-book accommodation months in advance and may have spaces.

Occasionally, the last-minute booker can get lucky: tour companies which pre-book in blocks will release unsold beds a few weeks or months before the relevant dates. If you call a few weeks before your trip, you may be lucky enough to bag some beds which have just been released.

Facilities

Stage	Place	Dormitory Beds	Private Rooms	Camping	Meals/Drinks	Food Shop	Transport
1a	Milngavie		▣		▣	▣	train, bus
1a (2.3 miles OR)	Blanefield				▣	▣	
1a (2.6 miles OR)	Strathblane		▣		▣	▣	bus
1a (1.5 miles OR)	Killearn				▣	▣	bus
1a/1b	Easter Drumquhassle		▣	◀			
1b/2a	Drymen	▣	▣		▣	▣	bus
2a/2b	Glenalva B&B		▣				
2b/3a	Balmaha	▣	▣		▣	▣	bus
3a/3b	Milarrochy Bay			◀			
3b/3c	Cashel			◀			
3c/3d	Sallochy		▣ OR	◀			
3d/4	Rowardennan	▣ OR	▣	OR	▣	▣	ferry

Stage	Place	Dormitory Beds	Private Rooms	Camping	Meals/Drinks	Food/Shop	Transport
5a/5b	Ardlui (OR; ferry)		✓	✓	✓		ferry
5b/6a	Inveraman		✓	✓	✓	✓	bus
6a/6b	Crianlarich (1 mile OR)	✓	✓		✓	✓	train, bus
6b/6c	Ewich House		✓				
6c/6d	Strathfillan		✓	✓	✓	✓	
6d/7a	Tyndrum	✓	✓	✓	✓	✓	train, bus
7a/7b	Bridge of Orchy	✓	✓	✓	✓		train, bus
7b/8a	Inveroran		✓	✓	✓		
8a/8b	Glencoe Mountain Resort	✓	✓	✓	✓		
8b/9	Kingshouse	✓	✓		✓		
9/10a	Kinlochleven	✓	✓	✓	✓	✓	bus
10/a/10b	Glen Nevis	✓	✓	✓	✓	✓	bus
10b	Fort William	✓	✓		✓	✓	train, bus

Food

*Loch Linnhe viewed fr...
Fort William town cen...*

Breakfast: for most trekkers, breakfast will be provided as part of the overn... package at B&Bs, pubs or hotels. Normally, this will be a 'Full Scottish' breakfast which... large helping of bacon, sausage, eggs, mushrooms and black pudding.

Lunch: most accommodation providers can prepare a packed lunch for you. Be... to request this the night before. Alternatively, on some stages, you can stop for lunch... pub or café along the route.

Evening meals: if your accommodation does not offer evening meals ther... staff will usually be able to recommend a pub or restaurant within walking distance. ... villages have a pub/inn, serving food and excellent beer. In fact, for many trekkers the... grub' and ale are highlights of the WHW: the craft beers available are some of Scotl... finest.

Self-catering: there are many grocery shops and small supermarkets that s... the WHW: these are listed in the route descriptions. Often the shops are small w... limited range of products but, as long as you are not too fussy, you should find p... to eat. However, if you are more particular, or you have specific nutritional requirem... you may wish to stock up on supplies in Milngavie or Fort William before setting o... the trek.

However, remember that food is heavy so, unless you are travelling very quickly, you... not be able to start the trek with all the food that you will require for the full distan... is much better to accept at the outset that you can only carry a few days' food th... exhaust yourself in the early stages of the trek by carrying too much. Many campers... only a small amount of food which they supplement with meals at pubs and cafés a... the way. It is sensible to carry dried food (such as pasta and rice): water is food's hea... component. Pre-packed freeze-dried meals for backpackers are an excellent c... because they are light and are prepared simply by adding boiling water.

cottish specialities

broath smokies: haddock smoked using a traditional process which dates k to the 19th century

ack pudding: a mixture of pork blood, animal fat, cereal (such as oatmeal) and ɔs. It is usually served at breakfast as part of a 'Full Scottish'

anachan: one of the finest Scottish desserts. It consists of layers of cream, oats raspberries

llen skink: a rough soup of smoked haddock, potatoes and onions

ɪggis: this is probably the most ɔus Scottish food and no trip to land is complete without trying ɪce. It is a complicated mixture of ɪp's liver, heart and lungs mixed oatmeal and spices and no two ɔes are the same. We think it is ime but it is fair to say that a great y people disagree!

Haggis, neeps and tatties

eps and tatties: 'neeps' are turnips and 'tatties' are potatoes. They are uently served together in Scotland, often with haggis

ottish tablet: a delicious concoction of sugar, butter and condensed milk h is a bit like fudge with a harder exterior

ɔvies: a hearty stew of potato, carrot, onion and meat which is often served with ɪkes

cotch Whisky

and is famous for its whisky or 'Scotch'. According to the Scotch Whisky Association, vord 'whisky' comes from the Gaelic 'uisge beatha', which means 'water of life'. The ɪst documented record of distilling in Scotland occurred in tax records from 1494.

nally, Scotch was made from malted barley but wheat and rye are also used. Today e are more than 130 whisky distilleries operating in Scotland: it is the greatest entration of whisky production in the world. By law, Scotch whisky must be aged in ls for at least three years. The minimum bottling strength is 40% alcohol by volume.

e are five different categories of Scotch:

ingle malt: made from malted barley at a single distillery. It is usually considered to ɔe a premium product

lended malt: a blend of different batches of single malt whisky, usually from different distilleries

ingle grain: made at a single distillery with malted barley and other malted or ɪnmalted cereals (such as wheat)

lended grain: a blend of different batches of single grain whisky, usually from ɪifferent distilleries

lended: a mixture of malt Scotch and grain Scotch

Travel

Travel to Scotland

By air: there are numerous airports in the UK and, in normal times, there are plenty domestic and international flights available. At the date of press, however, many servic were not operating due to COVID-19 and it was not clear if, or when, they would resu

Glasgow Airport is the closest airport to Milngavie, the WHW's S trail-head. The are usually flights to Glasgow from a variety of cities in the UK, mainland Europe North America. Glasgow city centre is only 15min from the airport by bus (every 30m www.firstbus.co.uk) or taxi: then from Glasgow city centre, there are trains and b to Milngavie or Fort William (see 'Travel to/from the primary trail-heads'). Furtherm Scottish Citylink bus 977 runs from Glasgow Airport to Ardlui (Stage 5a/5b; Inverarnan (Stage 5b/6a), Crianlarich (Stage 6a/6b) and Tyndrum (Stage 6d/7a). Sco Citylink bus 915 runs from Glasgow Airport to Balloch, Luss, Tarbet, Ardlui (Stage 5a OR), Inverarnan (Stage 5b/6a), Crianlarich (Stage 6a/6b), Tyndrum (Stage 6d/7a), Bridg Orchy (Stage 7a/7b) and Glencoe (Stage 8b/9; OR). You could also take a taxi from Glas Airport directly to Milngavie (30min; £20-30). Taxis are available just outside the air and there is a 20% discount if booked in advance: see **www.glasgowairport.com**. also operates to/from Glasgow Airport (**www.uber.com**).

Glasgow Prestwick Airport is also a good option. It has a number of flights from Europe. There are regular trains from the airport to Glasgow Central train sta (45min; **www.scotrail.co.uk**): then from Glasgow city centre, there are trains to Milng or Fort William (see 'Travel to/from the primary trail-heads'). Bus X77 runs from Glas Prestwick Airport to Glasgow Buchanan Street bus station (**www.stagecoachbus.co**

Edinburgh Airport has flights from a variety of cities in the UK, mainland Eu and North America. Trams run between the airport and the main Edinburgh train sta every 7min: from there, you can take the train to various destinations across th including Glasgow Queen Street station. In total, it takes about 1.5hr to travel by tran then train to Glasgow: then from Glasgow city centre, there are trains to Milngavie o William (see 'Travel to/from the primary trail-heads').

Inverness Airport has flights from a variety of cities in the UK. Stagecoach High Bus 11 runs every 30min between the airport and Inverness centre: then from Inve city centre, there are buses to Fort William (see 'Travel to/from the primary trail-head

By sea: there are numerous ferries to GB from the island of Ireland and mair Europe. The most useful services for the WHW are those from Northern Irelar Cairnryan (**www.stenaline.com; www.poferries.com**). Scottish Citylink bus 923 tr daily between the Stenaline ferry terminal and Glasgow Buchanan Street bus sta Although there are trains to Glasgow from Stranraer (which is only a few minutes b from Cairnryan), they take a long time. A quicker option is to take your own car o ferry and drive to Milngavie (2.25hr): see 'Travel to/from the primary trail-heads'.

ravel to/from the primary trail-heads

Those walking S-N will start at Milngavie which is only 7.5 miles from Glasgow city centre. Those walking N-S will start at Fort William.

By train: There are trains between Glasgow and both Milngavie and Fort William. Glasgow is well connected to the rest of the UK by train. For travel from nearby ports to Glasgow, see 'Travel to Scotland'. To check train times and buy tickets, **www.thetrainline.com** or **www.scotrail.co.uk**.

Milngavie: regular trains each day to/from both Glasgow Central station and Glasgow Queen Street station although you may have to change once (journey time 25-30min).

Fort William: daily trains to/from Glasgow Queen Street station (3.75hr with changes). There are also trains between Fort William and Milngavie (4.5hr with changes): these are useful if you have left a car or luggage at your start point.

By bus: there are numerous buses to Glasgow from around GB (**www.nationalexpress.com; www.uk.megabus.com; www.citylink.co.uk**). Long-distance buses within the UK often take longer than trains.

Primary Trail-head	Transport (Places in red have train stations)
Milngavie	▶ First bus 60A between Hope Street near **Glasgow Central Station** and Craigton Road, **Milngavie** (daily; 40min) ▶ First X10/X10A between **Glasgow** Buchanan Street Bus Station and **Milngavie** Station (daily; 40min) ▶ Glasgow Citybus 15 between **Glasgow** North Frederick Street/North Hanover Street and **Milngavie** Station (daily; 1hr) ▶ Trains to/from **Glasgow Central/Glasgow Queen Street** (multiple times every hour; 25-30min) and **Fort William**
Fort William	▶ Scottish Citylink 914/915/916 between **Glasgow** and **Fort William** via **Balloch**, **Luss**, **Tarbet**, **Ardlui**, **Inverarnan** (Stage 5b/6a), **Crianlarich** (Stage 6a/6b), **Tyndrum** (Stage 6d/7a), **Bridge of Orchy** (Stage 7a/7b) and **Glencoe** (daily; 3hr) ▶ Scottish Citylink 913 between **Edinburgh** and **Fort William** via **Crianlarich** (Stage 6a/6b), **Tyndrum** (Stage 6d/7a), **Bridge of Orchy** (Stage 7a/7b) and **Glencoe** (daily; 4.5hr) ▶ Scottish Citylink 919 between **Inverness** and **Fort William** (daily; 2hr) ▶ Trains to/from **Glasgow Queen Street** via **Bridge of Orchy** (Stage 7a/7b), **Tyndrum** (Stage 6d/7a), **Crianlarich** (Stage 6a/6b), **Ardlui**, **Arrochar/Tarbet**, **Garelochhead** and **Helensburgh Upper**. Also trains to/from **Milngavie**.

By car: you could park your car in Fort William or Milngavie and use public transp
to return to it at the end of the trek. In Milngavie, there is free parking at the train stat
(where there is CCTV) and along the road opposite the police station. Alternatively,
Premier Inn Hotels in Milngavie will normally let guests park while they hike the W
(free of charge except for a charitable donation). In Fort William, if you are staying
a hotel or B&B, they may let you park your car long-term for a fee. You can also be
reasonably priced parking in Milngavie or Fort William at **www.yourparkingspace.co.**

By taxi: there are plenty of taxi services in both Glasgow and Fort William, includ
those listed below. A taxi to Milngavie from Glasgow city centre takes about 25-30min
costs around £15-25.

Glasgow taxi operators:

► **Glasgow Taxis:** www.glasgowtaxis.co.uk; 0141 429 7070

► **Uber:** www.uber.com

► **GlasGo Cabs:** www.glasgocabs.co.uk; 0141 332 5050/0141 774 3000

Fort William taxi operators:

► **Lochaber Taxis:** www.lochabertaxis.com; 01397 706 070/01397 703 334

► **A&A Taxis:** www.fortwilliamtaxi.com; 01397 701 702

► **Alistair's Taxis:** www.alistairstaxis.co.uk; 01397 252 525

► **West Highland Taxis:** www.westhighlandtaxis.com; 01855 831 495

By private shuttle: some of the businesses which offer baggage transfer
'Baggage transfer') also provide transfers at the end of the trek. These include:

► **AMS:** www.amsscotland.co.uk; info@amsscotland.co.uk;
01360 312 840/07872 823 940

► **Baggage Freedom:** www.baggagefreedom.com; baggagefreedom@yahoo.com
07508 940 915

► **Travel-lite:** www.travel-lite-uk.com; info@travel-lite-uk.com;
0141 956 7890/07778 966 592

► **Ginger Routes:** www.gingerroutes.com; mail@gingerroutes.com; 07498 212 00

The WHW skirting the sh
of Loch Lomond (Stage

Public transport along the WHW

ere are numerous transport services that are useful to the WHW walker. Some stop places along the WHW itself and others serve towns and villages which are a short tance OR. In this book, we refer to all of these places (other than the primary trail-heads Milngavie and Fort William) as 'secondary trail-heads'. There is a list of them on pages and 46, together with details of the relevant transport options: these services can be eful if you need to abandon the trek for any reason or if you wish to skip a stage or two. ey can also assist if you are only intending to walk part of the WHW: see 'Hiking shorter tions of the WHW'.

ain: other than the train stations at the primary trail-heads (Milngavie and Fort liam), the only stations actually located right beside the WHW itself are at Crianlarich age 6a/6b; 1 mile OR), Tyndrum (Stage 6d/7a) and Bridge of Orchy (Stage 7a/7b). wever, there are also stations at some towns which are not too far away from the trail: xandria, Balloch, Helensburgh, Garelochhead, Arrochar/Tarbet & Ardlui (see the map page 42). From each station, there is easy access to Glasgow and Fort William. For ets and timetables, see **www.thetrainline.com**.

JSes: the key services operating close to the WHW are set out below. There are too ny bus services operating in the region to list them all.

Bus Service	Key Information (Places in red have train stations)
First X10/X10A	Daily buses between **Glasgow** Buchanan Street Bus Station and **Stirling** via **Milngavie** Station, **Strathblane** (Stage 1a; 2.6 miles OR) and **Killearn** (Stage 1a; 1.5 miles OR)
Scottish Citylink 914/915/916	Daily buses between **Glasgow** and **Fort William** via **Glasgow Airport** (915 only), **Balloch, Luss, Tarbet, Ardlui, Inverarnan** (Stage 5b/6a), **Crianlarich** (Stage 6a/6b), **Tyndrum** (Stage 6d/7a), **Bridge of Orchy** (Stage 7a/7b) and **Glencoe**
Scottish Citylink 976	Daily buses between **Glasgow** and **Oban** via Balloch, Luss, **Tarbet/ Arrochar**
Scottish Citylink 977	Daily buses between **Glasgow** and **Oban** via **Glasgow Airport**, **Balloch, Luss, Tarbet/Arrochar, Ardlui, Inverarnan** (Stage 5b/6a), **Crianlarich** (Stage 6a/6b) and **Tyndrum** (Stage 6d/7a)
Scottish Citylink 926	Daily buses between **Glasgow** and **Campbeltown** via **Glasgow Airport, Balloch, Luss, Tarbet/Arrochar**
Garelochhead Coaches 309	Daily buses between **Balmaha** (Stage 2b/3a) and **Alexandria** via **Drymen** (Stage 1b/2a). **Alexandria** is linked to **Glasgow** by train
Garelochhead Coaches 306	Daily buses between **Alexandria** and **Helensburgh**. **Alexandria** is linked to **Glasgow** by train. **Helensburgh** is linked by train to **Glasgow, Garelochhead, Tarbet/Arrochar, Ardlui, Crianlarich** (Stage 6a/6b), **Tyndrum** (Stage 6d/7a) and **Bridge of Orchy** (Stage 7a/7b)

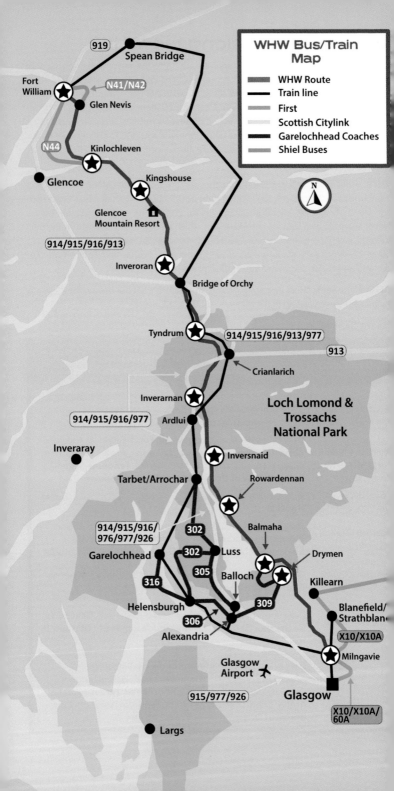

Bus Service	Key Information (Places in red have train stations)
Garelochhead Coaches 305	Daily buses between **Alexandria** and **Luss** via **Balloch**. **Alexandria** is linked to **Glasgow** by train
Garelochhead Coaches 302	Daily buses between **Helensburgh** and **Carrick Castle** via **Luss**, **Tarbet/Arrochar**. **Helensburgh** is linked by train to **Glasgow**, **Garelochhead**, **Tarbet/Arrochar**, **Ardlui**, **Crianlarich** (Stage 6a/6b), **Tyndrum** (Stage 6d/7a) and **Bridge of Orchy** (Stage 7a/7b)
Garelochhead Coaches 316	Daily buses between **Helensburgh** and **Garelochhead**: both are linked by train to **Glasgow**, **Tarbet/Arrochar**, **Ardlui**, **Crianlarich** (Stage 6a/6b), **Tyndrum** (Stage 6d/7a) and **Bridge of Orchy** (Stage 7a/7b)
Shiel Buses N44	Daily buses between **Kinlochleven** and **Fort William**
Shiel Buses N41/N42	Daily buses between **Glen Nevis Youth Hostel** and **Fort William** (July to mid-October). N41 does not run on Sundays
Scottish Citylink 913	Daily buses between **Edinburgh** and **Fort William** via **Crianlarich** (Stage 6a/6b), **Tyndrum** (Stage 6d/7a), **Bridge of Orchy** (Stage 7a/7b) and **Glencoe** (daily; 4.5hr)

rther information about bus travel:

t: www.firstbus.co.uk

sgow Citybus: www.westcoastmotors.co.uk

ttish Citylink: www.citylink.co.uk

elochhead Coaches: www.garelochheadcoaches.co.uk

l Buses: www.shielbuses.co.uk

ending into Glen
ch (Stage 5b)

Ferries: there are various cruises and waterbus/ferry services that operate, from time to time, on Loch Lomond. You could use them to skip stages by connecting with train/bus services on the W side of Loch Lomond; or you could use them to arrive at, or leave, the WHW; or perhaps consider a cruise simply to experience more of the loch. The services operating at the date of press, which would be of use to WHW trekkers, are set out below

Ferry Service	Key Information (Places in red have train stations)
Tarbet to Rowardennan	Cruise Loch Lomond (www.cruiselochlomond.co.uk; 01301 702 356); 45min crossing; April to November; £10 one way/£15 return
Tarbet to Inversnaid	Cruise Loch Lomond (www.cruiselochlomond.co.uk; 01301 702 356); 30min crossing; April to November; £10 one way/£15 return
Ardleish to **Ardlui**	Ardlui Hotel (www.ardlui.com); April to November; £5 each way; raise the ball as soon as you arrive at Ardleish to summon the ferry and the ferry will come at the scheduled time

Water taxis: Loch Lomond Leisure (www.lochlomond-scotland.com; 0333 577 0715) operates private-hire water taxi services on Loch Lomond. You could use them to skip stages along Loch Lomond or to access/leave the WHW. They are not cheap but could be cost effective for groups. Possible journeys (for up to 7 people) include:

▶ Rowardennan to Luss: £70; 15min

▶ Rowardennan to Inversnaid: £100

▶ Rowardennan to Balmaha £120

Taxis: there are many taxi businesses operating from towns and villages close to the WHW. They can often pick you up from the WHW, drive you to nearby accommodation and leave you back to the WHW the next morning. Some of them operate surprisingly from their hubs. Some of the useful services include:

▶ **Glasgow taxi services:** see 'Travel to/from the primary trail-heads'

▶ **Station Taxis (Milngavie):** www.stationtaxis.co.uk; 0141 942 4555

▶ **Ambassador Taxis (Milngavie):** www.ambassador-taxis.co.uk; 0141 956 2956

▶ **Drymen Taxi Services (Drymen):** 01360 660 077

▶ **Dacs Taxis (Drymen):** www.dacstaxis.com; 07868 534 494

▶ **Crianlarich Cars (Crianlarich):** www.247taxis.co.uk; 07787 788 360

▶ **Saltire Taxis (near Crianlarich):** www.saltireprivatehire.uk; 07387 982 976

▶ **West Highland Taxis (Glencoe/Kinlochleven/Fort William):** www.westhighlandtaxis.com; 01855 831 495

▶ **Levenside Taxi (Kinlochleven):** www.levensidetaxi.weebly.com; 07786 863 230

▶ **Fort William taxi services:** see 'Travel to/from the primary trail-heads'

Secondary trail-heads

Stage/Place (S-N)	Transport Options at Secondary Trail-heads (Towns in red have train stations)
1a Strathblane (2.6 miles OR)	▶ First bus X10/X10A to/from **Glasgow** Buchanan Street Bus Station, **Milngavie**, **Killearn** (Stage 1a; 1.5 miles OR) and **Stirling**
1a Killearn (1.5 miles OR)	▶ First bus X10/X10A to/from **Glasgow** Buchanan Street Bus Station, **Milngavie**, **Strathblane** (Stage 1a; 2.6 miles OR) and **Stirling**
1b/2a Drymen	▶ Garelochhead Coaches 309 to/from **Balmaha** (Stage 2b/3a) and **Alexandria**
2b/3a Balmaha	▶ Garelochhead Coaches 309 to/from **Drymen** (Stage 1b/2a) and **Alexandria**
3d/4 Rowardennan	▶ Cruise Loch Lomond ferry to/from **Tarbet**. Train and bus connections at Tarbet
4/5a Inversnaid	▶ Cruise Loch Lomond ferry to/from **Tarbet**. Train and bus connections at Tarbet
5a/5b Ardleish	▶ Ardlui Hotel ferry to/from **Ardlui**. Train and bus connections at Ardlui
5b/6a Inverarnan	▶ Scottish Citylink 914/915/916 to/from **Glasgow**, **Glasgow Airport** (915 only), **Balloch**, **Luss**, **Tarbet**, **Ardlui**, **Crianlarich** (Stage 6a/6b), **Tyndrum** (Stage 6d/7a), **Bridge of Orchy** (Stage 7a/7b), **Glencoe** and **Fort William** ▶ Scottish Citylink 977 to/from **Glasgow** via **Glasgow Airport**, **Balloch**, **Luss**, **Tarbet/Arrochar**, **Ardlui**, **Crianlarich** (Stage 6a/6b), **Tyndrum** (Stage 6d/7a) and **Oban**
6a/6b Crianlarich (1 mile OR)	▶ Scottish Citylink 914/915/916 to/from **Glasgow**, **Glasgow Airport** (915 only), **Balloch**, **Luss**, **Tarbet**, **Ardlui**, **Inverarnan** (Stage 5b/6a), **Tyndrum** (Stage 6d/7a), **Bridge of Orchy** (Stage 7a/7b) **Glencoe** and **Fort William** ▶ Scottish Citylink 977 to/from **Glasgow** via **Glasgow Airport**, **Balloch**, **Luss**, **Tarbet/Arrochar**, **Ardlui**, **Inverarnan** (Stage 5b/6a), **Tyndrum** (Stage 6d/7a) and **Oban** ▶ Scottish Citylink 913 to/from **Edinburgh**, **Tyndrum** (Stage 6d/7a), **Bridge of Orchy** (Stage 7a/7b), **Glencoe** and **Fort William** ▶ Trains to/from **Glasgow**, **Helensburgh**, **Garelochhead**, **Tarbet/Arrochar**, **Ardlui**, **Tyndrum** (Stage 6d/7a), **Bridge of Orchy** (Stage 7a/7b) and **Fort William**

Stage/Place (S-N)	Transport Options at Secondary Trail-heads (Towns in red have train stations)
6d/7a Tyndrum	▶ Scottish Citylink 914/915/916 to/from **Glasgow**, **Glasgow Airport** (915 only), **Balloch, Luss, Tarbet, Ardlui, Inverarnan** (Stage 5b/6a), **Crianlarich** (Stage 6a/6b), **Bridge of Orchy** (Stage 7a/7b) **Glencoe** and **Fort William** ▶ Scottish Citylink 977 to/from **Glasgow** via Glasgow Airport, **Balloch, Luss, Tarbet/Arrochar, Ardlui, Inverarnan** (Stage 5b/6a), **Crianlarich** (Stage 6a/6b) and **Oban** ▶ Scottish Citylink 913 to/from **Edinburgh, Crianlarich** (Stage 6a/6b), **Bridge of Orchy** (Stage 7a/7b), **Glencoe** and **Fort William** ▶ Trains to/from **Glasgow, Helensburgh, Garelochhead, Tarbet/Arrochar, Ardlui, Crianlarich** (Stage 6a/6b), **Bridge Orchy** (Stage 7a/7b) and **Fort William**
7a/7b Bridge of Orchy	▶ Scottish Citylink 914/915/916 to/from **Glasgow**, **Glasgow Airport** (915 only), **Balloch, Luss, Tarbet, Ardlui, Inverarnan** (Stage 5b/6a), **Crianlarich** (Stage 6a/6b), **Tyndrum** (Stage 6d/7a), **Glencoe** and **Fort William** ▶ Scottish Citylink 913 to/from **Edinburgh, Crianlarich** (Stage 6a/6b), **Tyndrum** (Stage 6d/7a), **Glencoe** and **Fort William** ▶ Trains to/from **Glasgow, Helensburgh, Garelochhead, Tarbet/Arrochar, Ardlui, Crianlarich** (Stage 6a/6b), **Tyndru** (Stage 6d/7a) and **Fort William**
8b/9 Glencoe (13 miles OR)	▶ Scottish Citylink 914/915/916 to/from **Glasgow**, **Glasgow Airport** (915 only), **Balloch, Luss, Tarbet, Ardlui, Inverarnan** (Stage 5b/6a), **Crianlarich** (Stage 6a/6b), **Tyndrum** (Stage 6d/7a), **Bridge of Orchy** (Stage 7a/7b) and **Fort William** ▶ Scottish Citylink 913 **to/from** Edinburgh, **Crianlarich** (Stage 6a/6b), **Tyndrum** (Stage 6d/7a), **Bridge of Orchy** (Stage 7a/7b) and **Fort William**
9/10a Kinlochleven	▶ Shiel Buses N44 to/from **Fort William**
10a/10b Glen Nevis Youth Hostel	▶ Shiel Buses N41/N42 to/from **Fort William**

The Highland Boundary Fault is visible from the summit of Conic Hill (Stage 2b)

osts & budgeting

vacations go, long-distance trekking in Scotland is relatively inexpensive. The walking
elf is free as no permits are required. The main components of daily expenditure are
d and accommodation/camping: approximate costs are set out below.

	Approximate Cost (subject to change)
Room in pub/inn	£35-70 per person sharing a double/twin room
B&B	£35-70 per person sharing a double/twin room
Bed in hostel	£20-30 per person
Bed in bunkhouse	£10-20 per person
Camping	£7-15 per person
Meal in pub/inn	£12-20
Packed lunch	£6-10
Beer (1 pint)	£5-6

eather

:land has famously green countryside and this beautiful greenery requires plenty of
er. The water is, of course, supplied by rain and Scotland's location near the Atlantic
an ensures that there is plenty of it: the island bears the brunt of many Atlantic fronts
hey make their way eastwards. Accordingly, it is likely that you will experience rain
ome point on the WHW. You might be lucky and walk in perfect conditions but you
uld always be prepared for wet weather, even in summer.

asionally, in summer, the sun in the Highlands can be strong. The heat saps your
gy but fortunately, the WHW has many forested sections where there is plenty of
de. However, on other parts of the trek, such as on the moors around Black Mount
ge 8a), there is no shade at all. Hot conditions reduce the distance that you can cover
a day. Dehydration and sunstroke are possibilities and you must carry more water than
nal.

The Highlands can also be windy and, in such conditions, you should exercise cauti
on the higher and more exposed parts of the WHW: in particular, take care in win
conditions on Conic Hill (Stage 2b) and on the high sections of Stage 9.

The WHW runs for 96 miles across Scotland and, at any given time, the weather on o
part of the trail can be completely different from the weather on another section:
example, it could be raining in Milngavie and sunny in Fort William or vice versa.

Always get a weather forecast before setting out. Many internet sites provide forecas
with a varying degree of reliability. The UK Met Office (**www.metoffice.gov.uk**) is one
the most reliable as it provides regularly updated localised forecasts for different plac
along the WHW, as well as specific mountain forecasts for the Highlands. It also provid
free of charge, an excellent smart-phone app that gives local forecasts.

Maps

In this book, we have included real maps for the entire WHW. Each stage has 1:25,0
scale maps produced by Ordnance Survey, GB's mapping agency. We believe that th
are the finest, and most detailed, maps available. They are perfect for navigating the WH
However, if you would also like sheet maps, there are a number of options:

▶ **OS Explorer 1:25,000:** the maps that are printed in this book are based on
  Explorer sheets. Six sheets are required to cover the entire WHW: sheets 348 (Camp
  Fells), OL38 (Loch Lomond South), OL39 (Loch Lomond North), 377 (Loch Etive & G
  Orchy), 384 (Glen Coe & Glen Etive) and 392 (Ben Nevis & Fort William).

▶ **OS Landranger 1:50,000:** five sheets are required to cover the entire WHW:
  (Glasgow), 57 (Stirling & the Trossachs), 56 (Loch Lomond & Inveraray), 50 (Glen Or
  & Loch Etive) and 41 (Ben Nevis).

▶ **Harveys West Highland Way XT40:** this single sheet 1:40,000 waterproof strip n
  covers the entire trek.

However, perhaps the best overall solution is to combine the real maps provided in
book with OS's excellent smart-phone app: it provides 1:25,000 maps for the whole o
and uses GPS to show your location and direction on the map. As the app's maps are
same as those provided in this book, they can be used together seamlessly. In the p
people often uploaded a series of GPS waypoints to their devices. However, because
OS app is so effective (showing both the WHW route and your actual location), in
opinion, there is now little point in bothering with GPS waypoint uploads. One mor
subscription to the app is only £3.99 so it is ideal for WHW walkers.

Paths and waymarking

The WHW normally follows clear paths and tracks. Often these are old drovers' tr
which highlanders used to lead their livestock to market. The WHW also makes good
of old military 'roads' built many centuries ago by soldiers and used to try to contro
Jacobite clans: these are wide and well maintained but the rock is hard underfoot. E
when it rains, these tracks are straightforward to walk upon although puddles do f
However, the narrower paths along the route can be muddy and slippery, particular
early spring and late autumn, or after sustained periods of rain. There are also some s
sections along minor roads and the WHW frequently crosses roads and farm tracks:
care at crossings, looking both ways for traffic.

Plenty of the countryside is farmland so there are numerous gates and stiles alonc
route. Like many routes in rural Scotland, the WHW has plenty of twists and turns

gotiates routes through farmland and villages. Consequently, the route has been remely well marked and navigation is usually straightforward: almost every junction s a white or yellow thistle waymark or a signpost. You will quickly get into a rhythm, king for the next waymark every time you pass one. In the route descriptions, we do not hlight every junction because the waymarking is so good: generally, we only mention ctions if they are particularly significant

if there are no waymarks. Bear in mind ough that waymarking is at the mercy of environment: for example, signs and ymarks are occasionally obscured by getation or destroyed by falling trees.

e terrain undulates regularly and hough gradients are normally not too ere, there are some short sections ich are very steep, including Conic (Stage 2b), some sections along Loch mond (Sections 3, 4 and 5) and the vil's Staircase (Stage 9). There are also ne longer climbs and descents on the W, particularly on the N half of the te.

A typical waymark

toring bags

en walkers from the UK travel to the WHW carrying only the gear that they will actually e on the trek. However, trekkers from further afield, and those who want to spend ne time elsewhere after the trek, will probably have additional baggage which they d to store while trekking. Normally, a hotel that you have stayed at near the start of trek will let you store bags until your return: check when booking. At the end of the , it is straightforward to get back to the start by train: see 'Travel to/from the primary -heads'. Alternatively, some businesses that offer baggage transfer can also store your lus luggage: see below.

aggage transfer

nesses offering baggage transfer services can transport your bags to your mmodation each night so that you only need to carry a small day-pack on the trail. spares you from the burden of having to carry a heavy backpack and enables you to more clean clothes and some luxuries. Most of the companies offering unguided s can organise baggage transfers. The following businesses offer baggage transfer ces along the entire WHW without a requirement to book an unguided tour:

Travel-lite: www.travel-lite-uk.com; info@travel-lite-uk.com; 0141 956 7890/07778 966 592

AMS: www.amsscotland.co.uk; info@amsscotland.co.uk; 01360 312 840/07872 823 940

Baggage Freedom: www.baggagefreedom.com; baggagefreedom@yahoo.com; 07508 940 915

Ginger Routes: www.gingerroutes.com; mail@gingerroutes.com; 07498 212 007

Sherpa Van: www.sherpavan.com; info@sherpavan.com; 01748 826 917

Fuel for camping stoves/Outdoor shops

Airlines will not permit you to transport fuel so campers who are flying to Scotland w
need to source it upon arrival, before setting out on the trek. There are outdoor shops
Glasgow, Tyndrum (Stage 6d/7a) and Fort William where you can buy fuel: methylat
spirits and standard screw-in gas canisters are normally available. Gas canisters are a
available at Inverarnan (Stage 5b/6a) and Crianlarich (Stage 6a/6b; 1 mile OR). At the d
of press, there was nowhere in Milngavie which stocked gas canisters so S-N trekke
would need to travel to Glasgow city centre to purchase them before starting the tr
Shops which stock gas canisters are listed below: it is wise to call in advance to ch
availability.

▶ **Glasgow: Tiso** (0141 248 4877); **Millets** (0141 375 0717); **Nevisport** (0141 332 40

▶ **Inverarnan (Stage 5b/6a): Beinglas Farm** (01301 704 281)

▶ **Crianlarich (Stage 6a/6b; 1 mile OR): Crianlarich Store** (01838 300 245)

▶ **Tyndrum (Stage 6d/7a): The Green Welly Stop Outdoor Store** (01301 702 089)
   Pine Trees Camping Park (01838 400 349)

▶ **Fort William: Nevisport** (01397 704 921); **Cotswold Outdoor** (01397 719 118); **E**
   Brigham (01397 706 220)

If you need petrol or diesel for a multi-fuel stove, there are service stations at the prin
trail-heads (Milngavie and Fort William) and at Tyndrum (Stage 6d/7a).

Midges

The midge or 'midgie' is a tiny biting insect which causes untold misery in the Scot
summer. Between June and September, they swarm in vast quantities, causing tempo
insanity in their human victims. They prefer some people to others but if they do like
taste of you, scores of itchy bites can result from exposure to a swarm. Mid-June to the
of August is normally the worst period. Because they do not like bright sunlight, they
more active at the start and end of the day or throughout overcast days. However, they
not normally a problem if there is wind.

To find out how bad the midge situation will be on any given day, you can check
midge forecast at **www.smidgeup.com**: it is created using data collected from mi
traps and weather stations.

There are some steps you can take to help you live with these horrific little beasties:

▶ **Cover your skin:** wear long trousers and long-sleeved shirts when they are ac
   Light-coloured clothing is apparently preferable. If the midgies are about, a mi
   proof face net can be a life-saver: they are inexpensive and you can buy them in sl
   along the WHW.

▶ **Keep moving:** it is harder for midges to catch you if you are on the move.

▶ **Stay inside at dusk and dawn:** if camping, it is wise to retire to your tent before
   make an appearance and do not get up too early. Use the bathroom before yo
   into your tent: from experience, we can tell you that a late evening toilet run can
   very painful experience!

Wear midge repellent: there are many different products but what works for one person may not work for another. Many contain the chemical DEET which is very effective but not very pleasant on your skin. Some people swear by Avon Skin So Soft (a moisturising oil which was not intended as an insect repellent) but we find it to be only slightly effective. Smidge (made by a Scottish business) is another popular product: it is DEET-free and you will find it in many shops along the WHW.

icks

s often the case in Europe, ticks are present in Scotland. They can carry Lyme disease or
-borne encephalitis so check yourself regularly. Remove ticks with a tick removal tool
aking sure that you get all of it out) and then disinfect the area.

rinking water

nking water will be one of your primary considerations each day. Even in Scotland, the
 can be hot: dehydration and sunstroke are always possibilities. Mains water in the UK
sually safe to drink. However, water is heavy and therefore it is not always possible to
t the day carrying all the water that you will need. Finding water on the trail is normally
ightforward though because there are pubs/cafés on many stages: many have outdoor
s and at others, the staff will normally fill your water bottles for free if you ask politely.

re are also plenty of streams, rivers and lochs along the way but bear in mind that
lability of water in streams may vary depending upon the season and the amount
ainfall over previous weeks and months. Although some do it, we would never
ommend drinking water from a river, stream or lake, in the UK, without first dealing
 possible contaminants including visible particulates (which sometimes give stream
er a brown colour), bacteria, viruses, protozoa (for example, giardia) and parasites.
re are a variety of possible ways to treat water:

Boiling is the traditional method. A rolling boil of 1min should kill everything in the water. However, it does not remove visible particulates so the boiled water will remain the same colour as when you found it, which can be off-putting. It also uses up a lot of fuel and takes time so is impractical.

Filtering usually removes visible particulates, working miracles by turning coloured water clear. It also removes 99.9% of bacteria, protozoa and parasites. Filters are often cheap and light. It is the quickest method of treatment so it is useful for long-distance routes. However, most filters cannot remove viruses so, if you are concerned about them, you will need to combine filtering with another method such as boiling, UV or chemical treatment.

Chemical treatment can remove bacteria, protozoa, viruses and parasites (each product is different so read the labels carefully). However, there are many disadvantages to chemicals: they do not remove visible particulates so the boiled water will remain the same colour as when you found it; water treated with chemicals usually has a taste; the water usually cannot be drunk immediately as chemicals take time to kill pathogens; and from a health perspective, consuming chemicals may not be good for you.

UV treatment kills bacteria, protozoa, viruses and parasites. However, it does not remove visible particulates so the boiled water will remain the same colour as when you found it: coloured water can be off-putting and the UV treatment is less effective f the water is not completely clear. The most common products are Steripens which are very light.

Perhaps the best single method for the WHW is filtering which turns the water clear a removes almost everything except viruses: although it is possible, you are unlikely encounter viruses in water along the WHW and some are prepared to drink water wh has only been filtered, running a small risk of virus contamination. However, we prefer combine filtration with UV treatment (using a Steripen): this removes or kills practic everything.

The actual effectiveness of individual products varies and is beyond the scope of this bc so do your research beforehand. However, it is worth noting that many products claim be 99.9% effective indicating that drinking water from wild sources can never be said be 100% risk free. You will have to weigh up the risks and make up your own mind. drink the water at your own risk!

	Visible Particulates	Bacteria	Virus	Protozoa	Parasites
Boiling	X	✓	✓	✓	✓
Filter	✓	✓	X	✓	✓
Chemical Treatment	X	✓	✓	✓	✓
UV Treatment (such as Steripen)	X	✓	✓	✓	✓

If, like many, you do decide to drink from natural sources in the Highlands then, as we treating the water, there are a few rules that you should follow to reduce further any

► Avoid water where there is evidence nearby of animals, especially cows or sh carcasses (of dead animals) or faeces can cause contamination
► Do not collect water downstream from buildings or grazing areas
► Preferably drink from moving water. The faster the better
► The bigger the river/stream the better
► Generally the higher the altitude the better

In the introduction to each section, we list the places where refreshments are avai along the route. It is good practice to fill up in the morning at your accommoda starting the day with at least 1.5 litres. Plan carefully so that you know where your water point will be.

Lambing

Between March and May, many ewes along the WHW will be lambing. Trekkers sh be particularly careful not to disturb the sheep at this time: do not bring dogs onto where there are pregnant ewes. If you spot any ewe in distress, or a lamb that appea have been abandoned, report it to the nearest farmer.

eer stalking

er in Scotland have no natural predators and shooting is used to help control the deer pulation and to generate some of the income required for the upkeep of Scottish ates. Stag stalking takes place between 1 July and 20 October. Hind (a female red deer) king takes place between 21 October and 15 February. Occasionally, there are access trictions on land where shooting is taking place (although this is unlikely to affect the te of the WHW). Whatever your opinion of shooting, you should respect any such trictions. For further information, see **www.outdooraccess-scotland.scot**.

alking with dogs

are generally permitted to take your dog on the WHW. The SOAC states that access ts apply to people walking dogs as long as their dogs are kept under proper control. wever, although dogs are normally permitted, certain fields may occasionally be ed to them during lambing season (see above): you should respect any diversions. thermore, although some accommodation may accept dogs, other places do not: ck in advance.

ler the SOAC, the key responsibilities for dog-owners are as follows:

Never let your dog worry or attack farm animals

Do not take your dog into fields where there are lambs, calves or other young farm animals

If you enter a field containing farm animals, keep your dog on a short lead or close at heel and keep as far as possible from the animals

If cattle react aggressively and move towards you, keep calm, let the dog go and take the shortest, safest route out of the field

Do not take your dog into fields of vegetables or fruit unless there is a clear path and keep your dog on the path

During the breeding season for ground-nesting birds (usually April-July), keep your dog on a short lead or close at heel in areas such as moorland, forests, grasslands, loch shores and the sea shore, to avoid disturbing the birds

In recreation areas and public places, avoid causing concern to others by keeping your dog close at heel or on a short lead

Pick up and remove your dog's faeces if it defecates in a public open place

Highland Cow (Stage 1a)

Equipment

Beginning the descent towa[rds] Glen Nevis (Stage 10a)

The long-distance trekker has no influence over challenges like weather and terrain [but] can control the contents of a pack carried on the trail. Some trekkers carry only a li[ght] day-pack, paying for a baggage transfer service to transport the bulk of their gear to t[heir] nightly accommodation: see 'Baggage transfer'. Many others, however, elect to carr[y] their own gear and it is fair to say that a lot of those people set off carrying equipm[ent] which is unnecessary or simply too heavy: this can result in injury and/or exhaust[ion] leading to abandonment. If you are intending to carry your own gear, then you sho[uld] give equipment choice careful consideration: it will be crucial to your enjoyment of [the] trek and the likelihood of success.

When undertaking any long-distance route, you should be properly equipped for [the] worst terrain and the worst weather conditions which you could encounter. On the W[HW] a key consideration is rain: you might not get any in practice but you should expe[ct it] when planning. In late spring, summer and early autumn, you should carry clothin[g to] combat cold, heat, sun and rain. Getting cold and wet in the hills is unpleasant and ca[n be] dangerous. Furthermore, even in Scotland, the sun can be strong.

However, the dilemma is that you should also consider weight and avoid carr[ying] anything unnecessary. The heavier your pack, the harder the trek will be. A trekker's [base] weight is the weight of his/her pack, excluding food and water. If you are not carr[ying] camping gear and cooking equipment, it is perfectly possible to get by with a base we[ight] of 5-6kg (13lb) or less. If you intend to carry camping equipment then, by investir[g in] some modern lightweight gear, you could start the trek with a base weight of 8-9kg (1[8lb] or less. Many people are quick to tell you that the lighter the gear, the greater the price [but] that is not always the case. While it is true that lightweight gear can be expensive, t[here] are also some excellent lightweight products which are great value. Tents, sleeping [bags] and backpacks are the three heaviest items that you will carry so they offer the big[gest] opportunities for weight-saving. But do not ignore the smaller items either as the we[ight] can quickly add up. So, if you can afford it, it is sensible to invest some money in [gear] before you go. The lighter your gear, the more you will enjoy the trek and the better [your] chance of success. Be ruthless as every ounce counts.

ecommended basic kit

ering of clothing is the key to warmth: warm air gets trapped between the
ers, acting as insulation. Merino wool or man-made materials are preferable:
y wick moisture away from the skin, keeping you warm. Do not wear cotton:
oes not dry quickly and gets cold.

Boots/Shoes	Good quality, properly fitting and worn in. Robust soles (such as Vibram) are advisable. For the WHW, trail-running shoes are adequate but many prefer boots with ankle support. Shoes/boots with a waterproof membrane (such as Gore-Tex) are a good idea.
Socks	2 pairs of good quality, quick-drying walking socks: wash one, wear one. Hand-wash them regularly, helping to avoid blisters. As a luxury, it is nice to have a third pair to wear in the evenings.
Waterproof jacket and trousers	A waterproof and breathable rain jacket is essential although it might never leave your pack. Waterproof over-trousers are also advisable.
Base layers	2 T-shirts and underpants of man-made fabrics or merino wool, which wick moisture away from your body: wash one, wear one. As a luxury, it is nice to have a third set to wear in the evenings.
Fleeces	2 fleeces. Man-made fabrics.
Shorts/ Trousers	2 pairs of shorts or walking trousers. Convertible trousers are practical as you can remove the legs on warm days. One pair of shorts and one pair of trousers is also a good combination in summer.
Warm hat	Always carry a warm hat. Even in summer it can be cold, particularly on windy days.
Gloves	Early or late season trekkers may wish to bring gloves.
Down jacket	Advisable in spring, autumn and winter when low temperatures are more likely, especially in the evening and early morning.
Camp shoes	It is nice to have shoes to wear in the evenings. Flip-flops or Crocs are a common choice as they are light. However, if you have comfortable hiking boots/shoes then you might consider not bringing camp shoes to save weight.
Waterproof pack liner	Most backpacks are not very waterproof. An internal liner will keep your gear dry if it rains. Many trekkers use external pack covers but we do not find them to be very useful: they flap in the wind and in heavy rain, water still finds its way into the pack around the straps (so you need an internal liner anyway).
Whistle	For emergencies. Many rucksacks have one incorporated into the sternum strap.
Head-light with spare batteries	You will need a flashlight if you are camping. And it is good practice to carry one for emergencies: it can assist if you get caught out late and enable you to signal to rescuers.

Basic first-aid kit	Including plasters, a bandage, antiseptic wipes and painkillers. Blister plasters, moleskin padding or tape (such as Leukotape) can be useful to prevent or combat blisters. A tick removal tool or card is also recommended.
Map and compass	For maps, see page 48. A GPS unit or a smart-phone app can be a useful addition but they are no substitute for a map and compass: after all, batteries can run out and electronics can fail.
Knife	Such as a Swiss Army knife. You are going to need to cut that cheese!
Sunglasses, sun hat, sunscreen and lip salve	Even in Scotland, the sun can be strong so do not set out without these items.
Walking poles	These transfer weight from your legs onto your arms, keeping you fresher. They also save your knees (particularly on descents) and can reduce the likelihood of falling or twisting an ankle.
Phone and charger	A smart-phone is a very useful tool on a trek. It can be used for emergencies. Furthermore, apps for weather, mapping and hotel booking are invaluable. It can also replace your camera to save weight.
Towel	If you are staying at campsites or bunkhouses, you will need a towel: lightweight trekking towels are good.
Toiletries	Campers will need to bring soap/shower gel: a small hotel-size bottle should be enough to last the trek, saving a lot of weight. An almost empty toothpaste tube will also save weight. For those who shave, shaving oil is a lightweight alternative to a can of foam/gel. Leave that make-up behind!
Ziplock plastic bag	A lightweight way of keeping money, passport and credit cards dry.
Ear plugs	Useful if staying in dormitories: you will thank us if someone snores!
Emergency food	Carry some emergency food over and above your planned daily ration. Energy bars, nuts and dried fruit are all good.
Water	See 'Drinking water' above. Hydration packs with tubes enable drinking on the move.
Toilet paper and trowel	Bring a backpacking trowel in case nature calls on the trail: bury toilet waste and carry out used toilet paper.
Backpack	Your backpack is one of the heaviest items that you will carry. The difference in the weights of various packs can be surprisingly large. 35-40 litres should be sufficient if you are not carrying camping gear. 45-60 litres should be adequate for campers. If you need a pack bigger than these then you are most likely carrying too much. Look for well-padded shoulder straps and waist band. Much of the weight of the pack should sit on your hips rather than your shoulders.
Midge repellent & face net	Midges are often problematic on the WHW (see page 50)

dditional gear for campers

nt: this is one of the heaviest things that you will carry so it provides a big opportunity
weight saving. Some 2-person tents weigh more than 3kg while others weigh less
n 0.6kg. The heaviest ones are normally built for extreme winter conditions and are
rkill for the normal WHW trekking season. The lightest ones are quite fragile but this
ot normally an issue on the WHW where campsites are often grassy. Although a few
mium brands charge a lot for their products and there are some very expensive tents
ne lightest end of the scale, these days there are plenty of lightweight tents available at
asonable price. Tents weighing 1 to 1.5kg often strike a good balance between price,
gevity and weight. Consider money spent here as an investment in your well-being
enjoyment of one of the world's great trails. Believe us when we say that a few kgs can
he difference between success and failure.

r tent should be waterproof to ensure that you stay dry during rainy nights. If you
going to use a very light tent then a footprint can be a good idea to protect its
e: 'footprint' is a trendy, modern word for what used to be known as a groundsheet.
etimes you can buy footprints specific to your tent model but we prefer to use a sheet
rvek which can be cut to size: Tyvek is extremely tough and is cheaper, and normally
ter, than most branded footprints.

nt Pegs: tent weights provided by manufacturers normally exclude the weight of
egs. The pegs actually provided with tents tend to be quite heavy and many trekkers
replacement ones which are lighter. Six heavy pegs can weigh as much as 240g while
ht pegs can weigh as little as 6g. There are many different types available these days
it is important to match the peg with the type of ground they will be used in. The
nd on the WHW is soft and normally grassy so it is usually easy to get pegs into it.
rdingly, they do not need to be too strong.

eping bag: each bag has a 'comfort rating': This is the lowest temperature at
h the standard woman should enjoy a comfortable night's sleep. There is also a 'lower
ort limit' which is for men. That may sound simple but it is not. Although all reputable
ing bag manufacturers use the same independent standard, the bags are not tested
e same place so there is a lack of consistency amongst ratings. Also, the ratings are
ned with an average man and woman in mind but every person is different: some
le get colder than others. The ratings should therefore be used as a guide only and it
e to choose a bag with a comfort rating which is a few degrees lower than the night
eratures that you will encounter. In June, July and August a bag rated between 5 and
is normally sufficient, depending on whether you 'sleep hot' or 'sleep cold'. In early
ate season, you may want something warmer. However, you do not want to bring a
nat is much too warm as that would add unnecessary weight to your pack.

tunately, with sleeping bags, price tends to be inversely proportional to weight. This
ely because the lightest bags are filled with goose/duck down which is expensive.
etic bags are also available but they are much heavier so down is a better choice for
ng. The disadvantage of down bags is that they can lose their warmth if they get wet
at is less likely if you have a good tent and pack liner. Our advice is first to decide
comfort rating you will require. Then choose the lightest bag (with that rating) which
n afford.

eping mat: this makes it comfortable for you to sleep on the hard ground and
tes you from the ground's cold surface. There are three types: air, self-inflating and
-cell foam. The advantages and disadvantages of each are set out below. For the
weight is normally more of an issue than warmth so we prefer air mats.

Sleeping Mat Type	Pros	Cons
Air mats: need to be blown up	Lightest Very comfortable Most compact when packed Thicker: good for side sleepers	Most expensive Hard work to inflate Can be punctured Less warm than self-inflating
Self-inflating mats: a combination of air and closed-cell foam. The mat partially inflates itself when the valve is opened	Warmest Very comfortable Quite compact More durable than air mats Firmness is adjustable by adding air	Heavier More expensive than closed-cell foam Can be punctured
Closed-cell foam mats	Light Least expensive Most durable Cannot be punctured	Not compact: needs to be strapped to the outside of your pack Least warm Least comfortable

Pillow: some use rolled-up clothing but we prefer inflatable trekking pillows w only weigh around 50g.

Stove: : you should choose a stove that uses a type of fuel which is available or WHW. Airlines do not permit you to carry fuel on planes so, if you are flying to Scot you will need to source fuel on arrival. Although methylated spirits are sometimes sto in outdoor shops, these days gas is more widely available (see 'On the Trail'). Mos stoves are designed to fit generic screw-on canisters (not Campinggaz) which are re available in the UK. Canisters for Campinggaz stoves (which are popular in France much harder to find so are not a good choice for the WHW. Multi-fuel stoves that petrol and/or diesel are useful though: there are service stations in Milngavie, Tyne (Stage 6d/7a) and Fort William.

Hundreds of different stoves are available, some more complicated than others. C the lightest ones are the most simple and often the most simple ones are rela inexpensive. If, like most campers, you will eat dried food such as pasta and rice then stove will need to do little more than boil water. A basic stove which mounts on to gas canister will therefore be adequate: such a stove should also be cheap and lightw (less than 100g).

Pots: if, like most campers, you eat dried food such as pasta and rice then you wi need one pot which will do little more than boil water. To save weight, go for the sm pot that you can get away with. For example, if you are travelling solo and planning freeze-dried backpacking meals then you would need nothing bigger than a 500-￼ pot. Titanium pots are usually the lightest but they are slightly more expensive. G lightest one that you can afford.

Fork/Spoon: we love Sporks! They have a spoon at one end and a fork at the They weigh a mere 9g and cost very little.

Safety

The old military road in Glen Falloch (Stage 6a)

a calm summer's day, the Highlands are paradise. But a sudden weather shift or an ry can change things dramatically so treat the hills with respect and be conscious of experience levels and physical capabilities. The following is a non-exhaustive list of mmendations:

The fitter you are at the start of your trip, the more you will enjoy the hiking.

Start early to avoid walking during the hottest part of the day and to allow surplus time in case something goes wrong.

Do not stray from the waymarked paths so as to avoid getting lost and to help prevent erosion of the landscape.

Before you set out each day, study the route and make plans based upon the abilities of the weakest member of your party.

Get a weather forecast (daily if possible) and reassess your plans in light of it. Avoid exposed routes if the weather is uncertain.

Never be too proud to turn back if you find the going too tough or if the weather deteriorates.

Bring a map and compass and know how to use them.

Carry surplus food and clothing for emergencies.

Avoid exposed high ground in a thunderstorm. If you get caught out in one then drop our walking poles and stay away from trees, overhanging rocks, metal structures nd caves. Generally accepted advice is to squat on your pack and keep as low as possible.

n the event of an accident, move an injured person into a safe place and administer ny necessary first-aid. Keep the victim warm. Establish your exact coordinates and, possible, use your cell-phone to call for help. The emergency number is 999. If you ave no signal then send someone for help.

When cooking on a camping stove, place the stove on the ground. Do not use it on a icnic table. We have witnessed a walker knocking over his stove and spilling boiling ater on his legs: this is a sure-fire way to end your trek.

General Information

Language: English is the main language.

Charging electronic devices: the UK uses a 3-pin plug. Visitors from outside the UK or Ireland will need an adapter. Some campsites, bunkhouses and camping barns facilitate the charging of electronic devices but this may not be possible at the more basic places. Some people carry their own portable charging devices.

Money: the UK uses Sterling (£). On the WHW itself, there are ATMs in **Milngavie** (Stage 1a), **Balmaha** (Stage 2b/3a), **Tyndrum** (Stage 6d/7a), **Kinlochleven** (Stage 9/10) and **Fort William** (Stage 10b). Off the main route, there are ATMs at **Blanefield** (Stage 1a; 2.3 miles OR), **Killearn** (Stage 1a; 1.5 miles OR) and **Crianlarich** (Stage 6a/6b; 1 mile OR). Credit cards are accepted almost everywhere.

Visas: citizens of the European Union, Australia, New Zealand, Canada or the US do not need a visa for short tourist trips to the UK.

Cell-phones: there is generally good network along the WHW. However, in the more remote parts, it can be difficult to get a signal. When network is available, it is likely to be a 3G/4G service enabling access to the internet from smart-phones. In the UK, roll-out of a new 5G network has begun.

International dialling codes: the country code for the UK is +44. When dialling from overseas, the 0 in UK area codes is omitted.

WiFi: nearly all hotels, pubs and B&Bs have WiFi (see Accommodation Listings). Some campsites and bunkhouses may not offer it.

Emergencies and rescue: rescue services are normally free and provided by unpaid volunteers. The emergency number is 999: ask for 'mountain rescue'.

Insurance: depending upon your nationality, any required medical treatment in the UK may not be provided free of charge so it is wise to purchase travel insurance which covers hiking.

Tourist Information: there are Visit Scotland tourist information centres in **Glasgow** (0141 566 4083) and **Fort William** (Stage 10b; 01397 701801). Information is also available from **Balmaha Visitor Centre** (01389 722100) and **Ben Nevis Visitor Centre** at Glen Nevis (01349 781401; info@highlifehighland.com). The following websites are useful too:

► **www.westhighlandway.org:** the official website for the WHW
► **www.visitscotland.com:** tourist information for Scotland
► **www.scotlandsgreattrails.com:** information on all of Scotland's Great Trails including the WHW
► **www.walkhighlands.co.uk:** general information about walking in the Highlands
► **www.lochlomond-trossachs.org:** website of the LLTNP
► **www.nts.org.uk:** website of the National Trust for Scotland

Wildlife

Red deer

...h of the fauna in Scotland is similar to that in other parts of the UK. There are foxes, ...gers, rabbits, red and grey squirrels, hedgehogs, mice, shrews, voles, stoats, weasels ...bats. However, it is the red deer (GB's largest land mammal) for which the Highlands ...most famous and you have a fairly good chance of spotting one along the WHW. ...w and roe deer are present too. More rare are pine martens and Scottish wildcats.

...e are also hares which are often ...used with rabbits but in fact they ...quite easy to tell apart: hares have ...nctive pointy faces and longer ears ...black tips). You may spot snakes too: ...rs (which are venomous) and grass ...es (which are not venomous). The ...ms and rivers of Scotland are famous ...heir trout and salmon and also support ...species such as otter. Beaver are now

...ent again after recent re-introductions. As regards domesticated animals, sheep are ...mely common. More interesting though are the long-haired, long-horned Highland ...e which most trekkers will be keen to photograph against the picturesque backdrop ...cottish mountain.

...y of the birds are also similar to those in other parts of the UK. However, there are ...pecies too such as black and red grouse (found on moorland). If you are lucky, you ...spot a ptarmigan which is related to the grouse: its plumage is white in the winter ...hanges to speckled grey/brown in summer. There are plenty of birds of prey too ...ding buzzards, kestrels and peregrine falcons. However, the jewel in the crown has to ...e golden eagle with its huge wingspan of up to 2.3m.

Plants and Flowers

Fox gloves

There are a variety of habitats along the WHW including much farmland and woodl where there are plenty of wild-flowers, particularly in spring. The bluebells in woodlands are a sight to behold in April/May. Gorse is also widespread and its yel flowers are a dominating feature of the countryside in spring. Anyone who walks thro a section of bright gorse will be struck by the mouth-watering coconut aroma. And course, there is the thistle, Scotland's national flower, which blooms between July September.

Thistle

Scotland's native trees include Scots pine, birch, alder, oak, ash, hazel, rowan, elm and hawthorn: most of these are easy to spot on the WHW. Unfortunately, these days, the Scots pine is rare: most of the conifers are the non-native species (such as Sitka spruce) found in the plantations created in the 20th century to increase GB's timber stocks (which had been greatly depleted during the two world wars). You will pass many of these conifer plantations on the WHW.

Frequently, the WHW crosses the wild heather moorland for which Scotland is famous. Common heather thrives on poor acidic soils like those found in Scottish peatlands. In fact, it is thought that 75% of the world's heather moorland is found i UK: it developed over thousands of years, as humans felled woodland to create gra for livestock. Red Grouse feed on the heather which flowers in August, giving the hill a vibrant purple hue.

Those walking the WHW in late summer and early autumn will find blackberries seem everywhere. Purple sloe berries (which grow on Blackthorn) are common too: they like giant blueberries but they do not taste like them! In fact, sloe berries are only palatable when added to gin.

Loch Lomond & the Trossachs National Park

The LLTNP was established in 2002 and was Scotland's first national park (the second being the Cairngorms National Park). It has a surface area of 1,865km² which includes the whole of Loch Lomond (Scotland's largest loch), the Trossachs (an area of wooded hills, lochs and glens E of Loch Lomond), 21 Munros (mountains which are over 3000ft) and two forest parks (Queen Elizabeth Forest Park and Argyll Forest Park). The highest mountain in the park is Ben More (1174m). The WHW travels through the park between Drymen (Stage 1b/2a) and Tyndrum (Stage 6d/7a).

The Highland Boundary Fault runs through the park: this is a geological line (dividing the lowlands from the highlands) which runs all the way across Scotland from Stonehaven in the E to the Isle of Arran in the W. N of the fault lie the mountainous highlands and S of it are the green, rolling lowlands: the two regions differ in geology, soil type and topography. Balmaha (Stage 2b/3a) lies on the fault, as does Conic Hill (Stage 2b) and there are good views of it from the summit: the fault runs across the islands of Loch Lomond just to the W.

Descending from the Devil's Staircase
towards Kinlochleven (Stage 9)

Route Descriptions

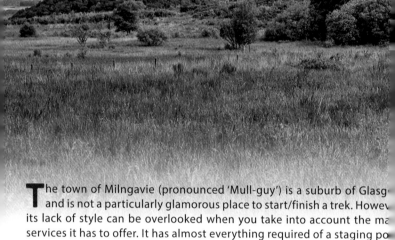

he town of Milngavie (pronounced 'Mull-guy') is a suburb of Glasg and is not a particularly glamorous place to start/finish a trek. Howev its lack of style can be overlooked when you take into account the ma services it has to offer. It has almost everything required of a staging po for a long-distance trek: good rail and bus connections, supermark for supplies, pubs and restaurants, comfortable hotels and safe places park. The only black mark is that it does not serve campers well: there no campsite and, at the date of press, there was nowhere to purchase canisters for camping stoves.

The WHW officially starts/finishes at the obelisk on Douglas Stre However, on the assumption that many trekkers will either arrive/dep by train or park at the train station, we describe the route from there. Th is a Tesco supermarket on the way from the station to the obelisk.

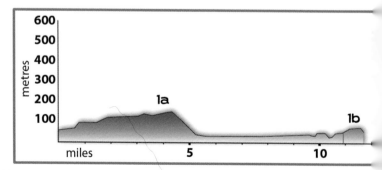

View of the peak of Dumgoyne (Stage 1a)

...om the obelisk, S-N hikers follow Allander Water N out of town. You soon ...ve the buildings behind as you follow a network of paths through forest. ...ortly after passing the pretty Craigallian Loch, you will strike out across ...en countryside: it is here that the joys of the WHW really begin (or end ...pending on your direction), with fabulous views across the Blane Valley ...wards the Campsie Fells and the attractive peak of Dumgoyne.

...ymen is a lovely place to spend your first night on the WHW. There is ...wide variety of places to stay (including a nearby campsite) and some ...od pubs and restaurants. There is also a small supermarket where you ...n stock up on supplies.

...e route is well marked and navigation is straightforward. The relatively ...terrain uses good paths and tracks. For S-N trekkers, Section 1 is a ...sibly gentle introduction to the trek.

		Time	Distance	Ascent S-N	Descent S-N
...age 1a	Milngavie/Easter Drumquhassle	4:45	10.9miles 17.5km	446ft 136m	512ft 156m
...age 1b	Easter Drumquhassle/ Drymen exit	0:15	0.8miles 1.3km	98ft 30m	52ft 16m

Supplies/Water:

Milngavie (Stage 1a) – supermarkets, shops, pharmacy & ATMs

Blanefield (Stage 1a; 2.3 miles OR) – convenience store & ATM

Strathblane (Stage 1a; 2.6 miles OR) – supermarket

Beech Tree Restaurant & Café (Stage 1a) – click and collect groceries (www.thebeechtreeinn.co.uk)

Turnip the Beet Deli (Stage 1a) – shop & free water refill

Killearn (Stage 1a; 1.5 miles OR) – supermarket, pharmacy & ATM

Gartness (Stage 1a) – honesty box (drinks, snack and ice cream)

Drymen (Stage 1b/2a; 0.5 miles OR) – the Village Hub shop (groceries and drinks); Spar supermarket

Refreshments/Food:

Milngavie (Stage 1a) – pubs, restaurants and cafés

Blanefield (Stage 1a; 2.3 miles OR) – The Wilsons coffee shop

Strathblane (Stage 1a; 2.6 miles OR) – Kirkhouse Inn

West Highland Way Campsite (Stage 1a; 0.5-1 mile OR) – café

Beech Tree Restaurant & Café (Stage 1a)

Turnip the Beet Deli (Stage 1a) – snacks and drinks

Oakwood Garden Centre (Stage 1a) – café/restaurant

Killearn (Stage 1a; 1.5 miles OR) – The Old Mill pub; Kitchen Window café

Drymen (Stage 1b/2a; 0.5 miles OR) – Clachan Inn; Drymen Inn; Buchanan Arms; Winnock Hotel; cafés

Accommodation:

Milngavie (Stage 1a) - hotels

Ardoch House (Stage 1a; 0.6 miles OR)

West Highland Way Campsite (Stage 1a; 0.5-1 mile OR)

Strathblane (Stage 1a; 2.6 miles OR) – Kirkhouse Inn

The Attic (Stage 1a; 2.1 miles OR)

Croftamie (Stage 1a; 1.8 miles OR): Croftburn B&B

Easter Drumquhassle (Stage 1a/1b) – Drymen Camping; Altquhur Byre B&B

Drymen (Stage 1b/2a; 0.5 miles OR) – bunkhouse, pubs, B&Bs and hotels

Escape/Access:

Milngavie (Stage 1a) – bus/train

Strathblane (Stage 1a; 2.6 miles OR) – bus

Gallearn (Stage 1a; 1.5 miles OR) - bus

Drymen (Stage 1b/2a; 0.5 miles OR) - bus

The WHW heading N to Drymen (Stage 1a)

S-N

To reach the start from **Milngavie station**, head N through an underpass to arrive in the town centre. Soon, TL and walk along **Station Road** until you reach the obelisk marking the official start of the WHW. Alternatively, TL before the underpass to head to the **Tesco supermarket**: from the S end of the supermarket's car park, head N on **Main Street** to reach the obelisk.

Stage 1a: Milngavie to Easter Drumquhassle

S From the obelisk, pass under the WHW banner and descend past a series of metal plaques (depicting points of interest along the trek). Afterwards, bear right and follow WHW signs along a tree-lined path. 5min later, TL. Shortly afterwards, TR at a junction.

(1) 0:15: TR away from **Allander Water**. 5min later, TL at a fork (no signpost).

(2) 0:55: TL down a lane. Shortly afterwards, TR on a path. Keep SH past **Craigallian Loch**.

(3) 1:25: TR at a junction.

(4) 1:35: Reach a junction: keep SH to continue on the WHW or TR on the John Muir Way to head to **Blanefield** or **Strathblane**. A few minutes later, TL along the B821 to continue on the WHW: alternatively, TR along the road to head to **Ardoch House**, **Blanefield** or **Strathblane**. 5-10min later, TR on a path and enjoy the first great views of the WHW.

(5) 2:00: TL at a fork to continue on the WHW: alternatively, TR for the **West Highland Way Campsite**. Shortly afterwards, TL again.

(6) 2:30: TL onto another path. 20min later, pass a path on the right which heads to **Glengoyne Distillery**: tours and whisky tasting (www.glengoyne.com).

(7) 3:05: Just after **Beech Tree Restaurant & Café**, cross a road and keep SH on a path. 15min later, pass **Turnip the Beet Deli**: nearby, you can TR and head NE on **Drumbeg Loan** if you wish to go to **Killearn**.

(8) 3:30: At **Oakwood Garden Centre**, TR onto a lane. Shortly afterwards, TL and go through a gate.

(9) 4:15: TL down a road. Shortly afterwards, pass through the hamlet of **Gartness** where there is an honesty box.

F 4:45: Arrive at **Altquhur Byre B&B** at **Easter Drumquhassle**. Just afterwards, reach **Drymen Camping**.

N-S

Stage 1a: Easter Drumquhassle to Milngavie

F Continue SE along the road. 25min later, pass through the hamlet of **Gartness** where there is an honesty box.

(9) 0:30: A few minutes later, TR. 35min later, keep SH across the B834: alternatively, TL to head to **Killearn**.

(8) 1:15: At **Oakwood Garden Centre**, go through a gate and TR onto a lane. Shortly afterwards, TL, leaving the lane. 10min later, pass **Turnip the Beet Deli**: nearby you can TL and head NE on **Drumbeg Loan** if you wish to go to **Killearn**.

(7) 1:40: Cross a road and keep SH past **Beech Tree Restaurant & Café**. 15min later, pass a path on the left which heads to **Glengoyne Distillery**: tours and whisky tasting (www.glengoyne.com).

(6) 2:15: TR onto another path.

(5) 2:45: TR to continue on the WHW: alternatively, keep SH for **West Highland**

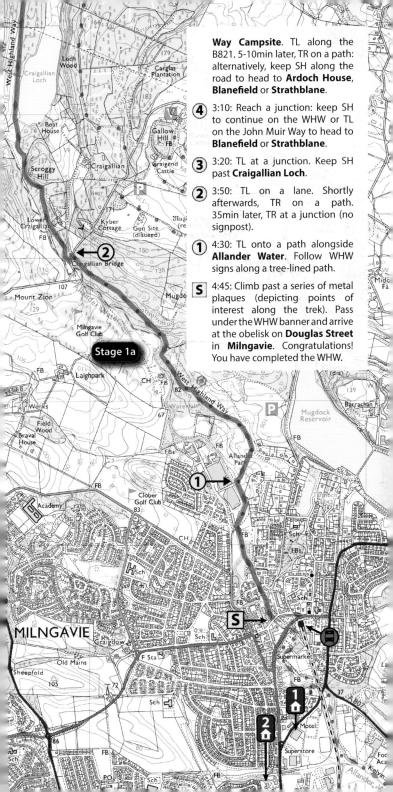

Way Campsite. TL along the B821. 5-10min later, TR on a path: alternatively, keep SH along the road to head to **Ardoch House**, **Blanefield** or **Strathblane**.

④ 3:10: Reach a junction: keep SH to continue on the WHW or TL on the John Muir Way to head to **Blanefield** or **Strathblane**.

③ 3:20: TL at a junction. Keep SH past **Craigallian Loch**.

② 3:50: TL on a lane. Shortly afterwards, TR on a path. 35min later, TR at a junction (no signpost).

① 4:30: TL onto a path alongside **Allander Water**. Follow WHW signs along a tree-lined path.

Ⓢ 4:45: Climb past a series of metal plaques (depicting points of interest along the trek). Pass under the WHW banner and arrive at the obelisk on **Douglas Street** in **Milngavie**. Congratulations! You have completed the WHW.

Stage 1a

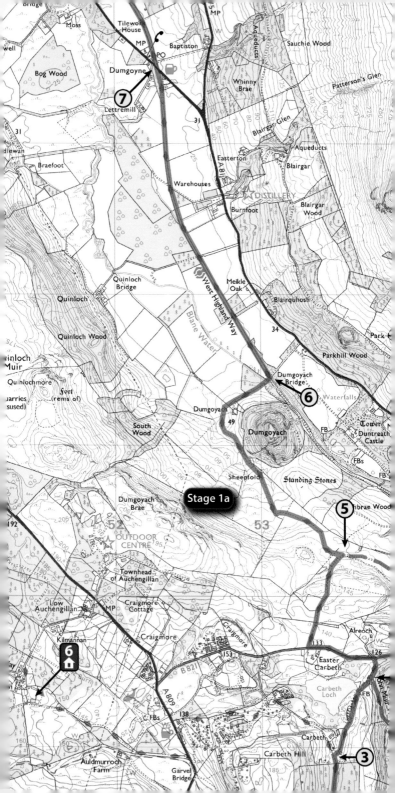

Stage 1a

S-N

Stage 1b: Easter Drumquhassle to Drymen exit

S Keep N along the road. 15min later, pass **Mulberry Lodge**.

F 0:15: Just afterwards, reach a **bridge**. TR on a path to start **Stage 2a** (avoiding Drymen). Alternatively, keep SH across the bridge to head to **Drymen** (0.5 miles OR): at the next junction, cross the road and pick up a path.

N-S

To reach **F** from the centre of **Drymen**, head E on **Gartness Road**. Cross the A811 and continue on **Gartness Road**. 10-15min from Drymen, reach the **bridge** at **F**

Stage 1b: Drymen exit to Easter Drumquhassle

F Head S along the road, passing **Mulberry Lodge**.

S 0:15: Arrive at **Drymen Camping** at **Easter Drumquhassle**. Just afterwards, reach **Altquhur Byre B&B**.

The obelisk at the start/finish of the WHW in Milngavie

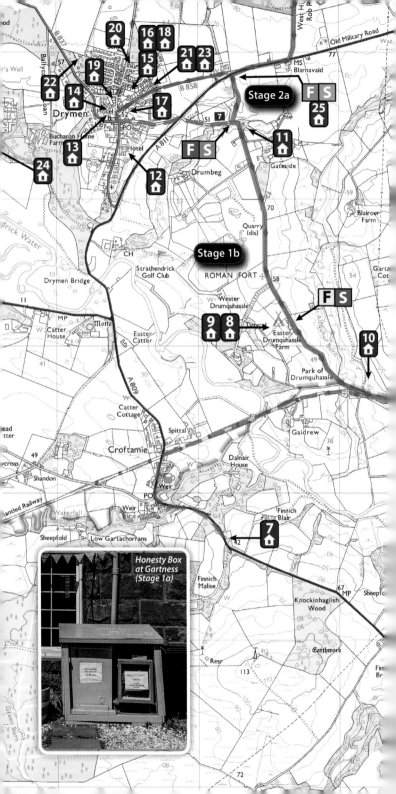

Stage 2a

Stage 1b

ROMAN FORT

Honesty Box
at Gartness
(Stage 1a)

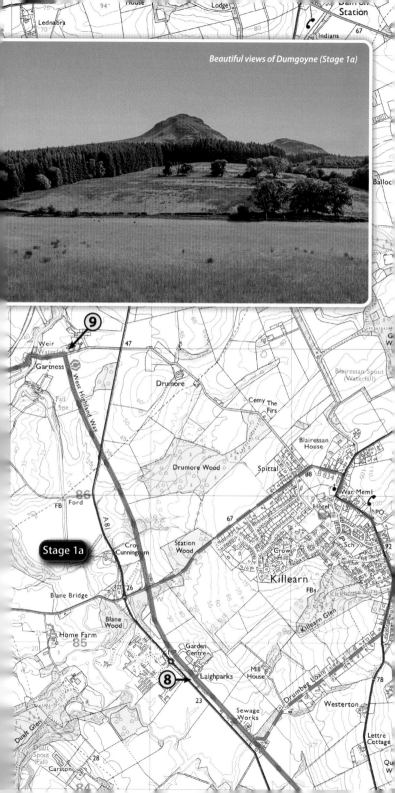

Beautiful views of Dumgoyne (Stage 1a)

Stage 1a

Drymen exit/Balmaha

2

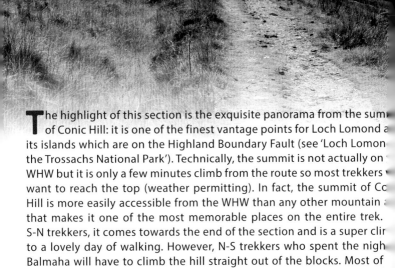

The highlight of this section is the exquisite panorama from the sum of Conic Hill: it is one of the finest vantage points for Loch Lomond a its islands which are on the Highland Boundary Fault (see 'Loch Lomon the Trossachs National Park'). Technically, the summit is not actually on WHW but it is only a few minutes climb from the route so most trekkers want to reach the top (weather permitting). In fact, the summit of Co Hill is more easily accessible from the WHW than any other mountain a that makes it one of the most memorable places on the entire trek. S-N trekkers, it comes towards the end of the section and is a super clir to a lovely day of walking. However, N-S trekkers who spent the nigh Balmaha will have to climb the hill straight out of the blocks. Most of rest of Section 2 takes place in the lovely Garadhban Forest but, even th the views of Conic Hill dominate.

The climb of Conic Hill, from either direction, is steep and tiring. The rc of the WHW is exposed near the summit and should be avoided du

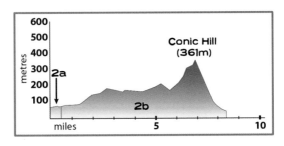

76

Views of Loch Lomond from the WHW on Conic Hill (Stage 2b)

riods of high wind, low visibility or bad weather. You can avoid the hill using the Milton Variant (see page 80).

maha is perched right on the edge of Loch Lomond and is a beautiful ce for an overnight stop. There are some good places to stay including Bs, a hotel and a bunkhouse. You can eat at the Oak Tree Inn (which s some of the best local beers on the WHW) or Perch Café & Restaurant ich is a short distance E of the centre. For N-S trekkers, Drymen is a ely place to spend your last night on the WHW. There is a wide variety accommodation (including a nearby campsite) and some pubs and taurants. There is also a small supermarket where you can stock up on plies.

e route is generally well marked and navigation is straightforward. S-N kers should take care when descending Conic Hill towards Balmaha: path is steep with some loose rock.

		Time	Distance	Ascent S-N	Descent S-N
age 2a	Drymen exit/ Glenalva B&B	0:15	0.5miles 0.8km	59ft 18m	0ft 0m
age 2b	Glenalva B&B/ Balmaha	4:00	7.8miles 12.5km	1253ft 382m	1440ft 439m

Supplies/Water:

Drymen (Stage 1b/2a; 0.5 miles OR) – the Village Hub shop (groceries and drinks); Spar supermarket

Honesty box (Stage 2b) - water

Balmaha (Stage 2b/3a) – village shop (basic groceries) & ATM

Refreshments/Food:

Drymen (Stage 1b/2a; 0.5 miles OR) – Clachan Inn; Drymen Inn; Buchanan Arms; Winnock Hotel; cafés

Balmaha (Stage 2b/3a) – Oak Tree Inn; St Mocha Coffee Shop & Ice Cream Parlour; Perch Café and Restaurant

Balmaha sits right on the shore of Loch Lomond

Accommodation:

Drymen (Stage 1b/2a; 0.5 miles OR) – bunkhouse, pubs, B&Bs and hotels

Glenalva B&B (Stage 2a/2b)

Balmaha (Stage 2b/3a) – hotel, B&Bs and bunkhouse

Escape/Access:

Drymen (Stage 1b/2a; 0.5 miles OR) - bus

Balmaha (Stage 2b/3a) - bus

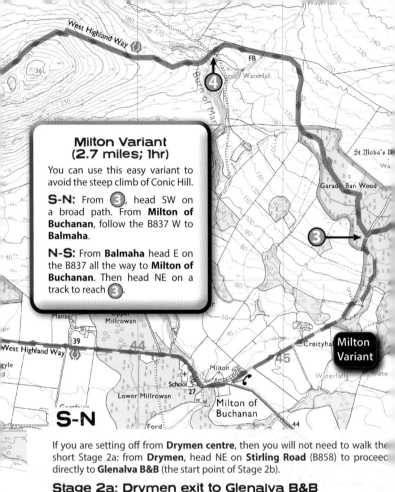

Milton Variant
(2.7 miles; 1hr)

You can use this easy variant to avoid the steep climb of Conic Hill.

S-N: From ③, head SW on a broad path. From **Milton of Buchanan**, follow the B837 W to **Balmaha**.

N-S: From **Balmaha** head E on the B837 all the way to **Milton of Buchanan**. Then head NE on a track to reach ③.

S-N

If you are setting off from **Drymen centre**, then you will not need to walk the short Stage 2a: from **Drymen**, head NE on **Stirling Road** (B858) to proceed directly to **Glenalva B&B** (the start point of Stage 2b).

Stage 2a: Drymen exit to Glenalva B&B

S From the bridge, head N on a path.

F 0:10: Arrive at a road (**A811**) near **Glenalva B&B**.

Stage 2b: Glenalva B&B to Balmaha

S Head E alongside the **A811**. After 5min, pass an **honesty box** (water). A few minutes later, TL on a path.

① 0:25: TL at a junction. 20min later, TL down a lane. Just afterwards, TR into a car park: keep SH past an information board and descend on a track (no signpost). Keep SH through forest, ignoring offshoots. Soon you will see **Loch Lomond**.

② 1:15: TR at a junction.

③ 1:35: Reach a broad junction. Head NW to continue on the main WHW (which climbs Conic Hill) or TL for the **Milton Variant** (see box).

④ 2:20: Keep SH at a crossroads, descending on a rocky path. Shortly, cross a bridge over a stream and then climb steeply. Eventually, the path runs along the N side of **Conic Hill (361m)**: see page 82.

F 4:00: Head S through a car park (passing a visitor centre and toilets). Shortly afterwards, reach the shore of Loch Lomond at **Balmaha**.

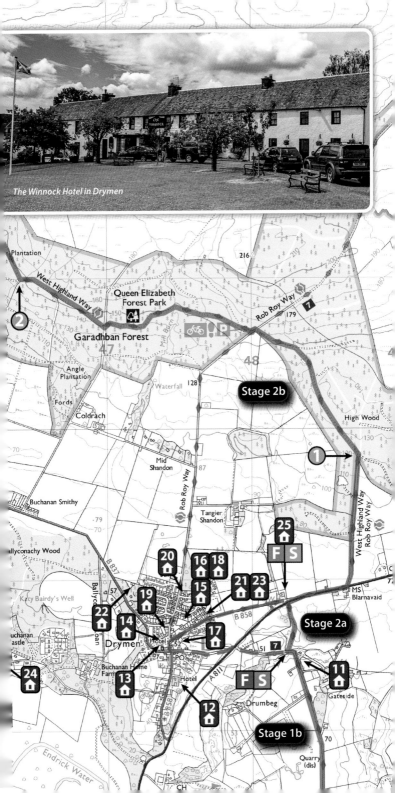

The Winnock Hotel in Drymen

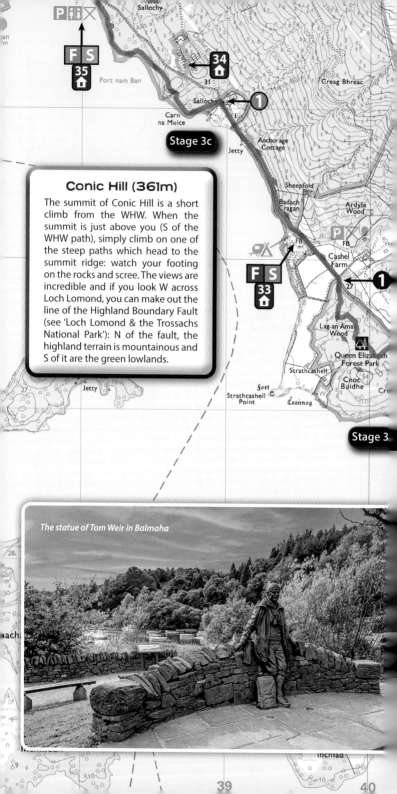

Conic Hill (361m)

The summit of Conic Hill is a short climb from the WHW. When the summit is just above you (S of the WHW path), simply climb on one of the steep paths which head to the summit ridge: watch your footing on the rocks and scree. The views are incredible and if you look W across Loch Lomond, you can make out the line of the Highland Boundary Fault (see 'Loch Lomond & the Trossachs National Park'): N of the fault, the highland terrain is mountainous and S of it are the green lowlands.

Stage 3

The statue of Tom Weir in Balmaha

39   40

Stage 2b: Balmaha to Glenalva B&B

F From Balmaha, head N through the car park for **Queen Elizabeth Forest Park** (passing a visitor centre and toilets). Climb generally NE through the forest on paths. After a long, steep climb, the path runs along the N side of **Conic Hill (361m)**: see box. Soon, descend E.

4 1:40: Cross a bridge over a stream. Shortly afterwards, climb a rocky path and keep SH at a crossroads.

3 2:25: Arrive at a junction: the path arriving from the S is the **Milton Variant** (see page 80). Head E on a path to continue on the WHW.

2 2:45: TL at a junction and continue E through forest, ignoring offshoots. After 25min, head through a car park. Then TL on a lane. Just afterwards, TR.

1 3:35: TR at a junction. 20min later, TR and head W alongside the **A811**. Pass an **honesty box** (water).

5 4:00: 5min later, reach **Glenalva B&B**. Head W on the **B858** to head to **Drymen** (15min). Alternatively, for **Stage 2a**, head S on a path which starts on the S side of the **A811**.

Stage 2a: Glenalva B&B to Drymen exit

From **Glenalva B&B**, head S on a path which starts on the S side of the **A811**.

0:10: Arrive at a road beside a bridge.

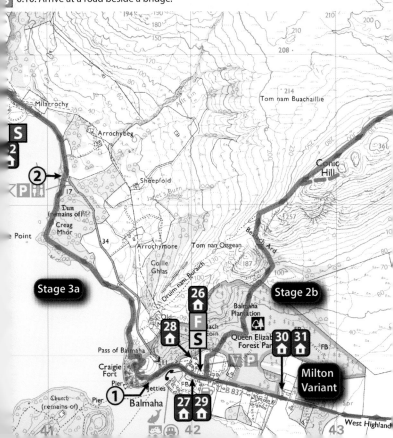

3 Balmaha/Rowardennan

Loch Lomond is Scotland's largest loch and the WHW follows the shores of it for about 21 miles in total: Sections 3, 4 and 5 of the tr For S-N trekkers, Section 3 is an excellent introduction to the delights a difficulties of walking alongside the loch. The delights are fairly obvio seemingly never-ending waters of the deepest blue, flanked by beauti indigenous forest and broad highland peaks. As you head N, the lo narrows and the quality of the scenery improves gradually: so, as y progress through Sections 3, 4 and 5, the scenery continues to impress

The difficulties are not so apparent because, on paper, the path appe relatively innocuous: level and without any sustained climbs. The ma however, only tell part of the story and disguise the fact that the ro along Loch Lomond is arguably the most technically challenging part the WHW: the paths are often narrow, winding and covered with ro and rocks which are slippery when wet. On some sections, the ro undulates relentlessly and can be muddy after rain. Fortunately, 7.9 miles of Section 3 are some of the easiest along the loch, giving trekkers a chance to warm up before the more challenging sections N

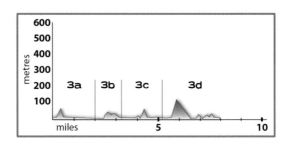

...wardennan (Sections 4 and 5). For N-S trekkers, the best sections of Loch ...mond will be behind you but at least you will have the excellent Conic ...l to look forward to on Section 2.

...s section of the WHW is within the LLTNP and wild camping is generally ...ohibited. However, there are plenty of lovely campsites along the way. ...thermore, there is one LLTNP permit area on Stage 3d where you ...n wild camp if you have obtained a permit in advance: the setting is ...nderful. Rowardennan (Stage 3d/4a) has the most accommodation ...tions. Rowardennan Hotel has a beautiful location right next to the ...h and a welcoming pub, the Clansman Bar. Rowardennan Lodge Youth ...stel and Ben Lomond Bunkhouse are located about 0.5 miles N of ...wardennan, along the route of Section 4.

...e route is well marked and navigation is straightforward.

		Time	Distance	Ascent S-N	Descent S-N
...age 3a	Balmaha/ Milarrochy Bay	0:45	2.0miles 3.2km	171ft 52m	180ft 55m
...age 3b	Milarrochy Bay/ Cashel	0:30	1.3miles 2.1km	98ft 30m	69ft 21m
...age 3c	Cashel/Sallochy	0:45	1.9miles 3.1km	164ft 50m	194ft 59m
...age 3d	Sallochy/ Rowardennan	1:30	2.7miles 4.3km	456ft 139m	417ft 127m

Supplies/Water:

Balmaha (Stage 2b/3a) – village shop (groceries) & ATM

Rowardennan Lodge Youth Hostel (0.5 miles N of Rowardennan on Section 4) – shop (basic provisions, confectionery and drinks)

Refreshments/Food:

Balmaha (Stage 2b/3a) – Oak Tree Inn; St Mocha Coffee Shop & Ice Cream Parlour; Perch Café and Restaurant

Rowardennan (Stage 3d/4) - Clansman Bar at Rowardennan Hotel

Rowardennan Lodge Youth Hostel (0.5 miles N of Rowardennan on Section 4)

Loch Lomond at Rowardennan (Stage 3d/4)

Accommodation:

Balmaha (Stage 2b/3a) – Hotel, B&Bs and bunkhouse

Milarrochy Bay Camping & Caravanning Club Site (Stage 3a/3b)

Cashel Campsite (Stage 3b/3c)

The Shepherd's House B&B (Stage 3c; 0.2 miles OR)

Sallochy Campsite (Stage 3c/3d)

LLTNP permit area (Stage 3d) – see 'Wild camping'

Rowardennan Hotel (Stage 3d/4)

Rowardennan Lodge Youth Hostel & Ben Lomond Bunkhouse
(0.5 miles N of Rowardennan on Section 4)

Escape/Access:

Balmaha (Stage 2b/3a) - bus

Rowardennan (Stage 3d/4) – ferry/water-taxi

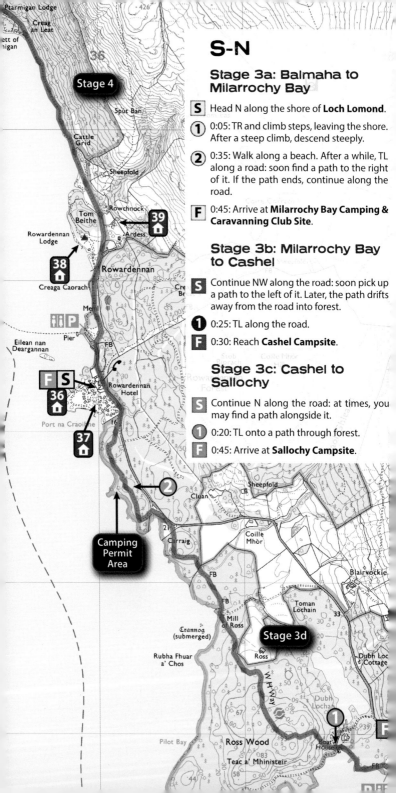

S–N

Stage 3a: Balmaha to Milarrochy Bay

S Head N along the shore of **Loch Lomond**.

1 0:05: TR and climb steps, leaving the shore. After a steep climb, descend steeply.

2 0:35: Walk along a beach. After a while, TL along a road: soon find a path to the right of it. If the path ends, continue along the road.

F 0:45: Arrive at **Milarrochy Bay Camping & Caravanning Club Site**.

Stage 3b: Milarrochy Bay to Cashel

S Continue NW along the road: soon pick up a path to the left of it. Later, the path drifts away from the road into forest.

1 0:25: TL along the road.

F 0:30: Reach **Cashel Campsite**.

Stage 3c: Cashel to Sallochy

S Continue N along the road: at times, you may find a path alongside it.

1 0:20: TL onto a path through forest.

F 0:45: Arrive at **Sallochy Campsite**.

S-N

Stage 3d: Sallochy to Rowardennan

From the N end of **Sallochy Campsite**, follow a path along the shore of the loch.

0:10: TR at a junction and climb steeply.

1:10: Pass a **LLTNP permit area**: you are permitted to camp if you have a permit (see 'Wild camping'). 10-15min later, TL on a path alongside a minor road.

1:30: Arrive at **Rowardennan Hotel**. To head to the youth hostel and bunkhouse, start following the Section 4 directions.

N-S

Stage 3d: Rowardennan to Sallochy

From **Rowardennan Hotel**, head SE alongside a road. 5min later, TR on a path heading into forest.

0:20: Pass a **LLTNP permit area**: you are permitted to camp if you have a permit (see 'Wild camping').

1:20: After descending steeply, TL at a junction.

1:30: Arrive at **Sallochy Campsite**.

Stage 3c: Sallochy to Cashel

From **Sallochy Campsite**, head SE on a path through the forest.

0:25: TR along the road: at times, you may find a path alongside it.

0:45: Reach **Cashel Campsite**.

Stage 3b: Cashel to Milarrochy Bay

From **Cashel Campsite**, head SE along the road.

0:05: TR onto a path which heads into forest. Later, the path returns to the road and continues alongside it. At times, continue along the road itself.

0:30: Arrive at **Milarrochy Bay Camping & Caravanning Club Site**.

Stage 3a: Milarrochy Bay to Balmaha

Head SE along the road: soon find a path to the left of it.

0:10: Bear right onto a beach: walk along it for a short distance and soon pick up a path again. After 25min, climb steeply and then descend (back towards the shore of the loch).

0:40: After descending steps, TL.

0:45: Arrive at **Balmaha**.

Sallochy Campsite (Stage 3c/3d)

4 Rowardennan/ Inversnaid

Although you remain almost entirely within forest, the wonder views of Loch Lomond continue. Between the lovely indigenous tre the sublime scenery is sometimes visible only in tantalising glimps heightening your desire for an opportunity to admire the landscape fro more open vantage point. Fortunately, such opportunities arise frequer because (on the Low Route) you regularly pass beaches and coves wh are only a stone's throw from the path: you only need to take a few step find yourself at the water's edge, gazing across at the mountains on th shore. The loch is narrower here than further S and the proximity to the side of it makes the scenery more dramatic.

There are two different WHW routes shown on the OS map: one runs ri along the edge of the loch (the '**Low Route**') and the other travels para to the loch, slightly further inland (the '**High Route**'). At the date of pr the signposts on the ground directed WHW trekkers along the Low Ro and the High Route was not actually signposted. Accordingly, we desc the Low Route as the main path and the High Route as an optional vari.

The Low Route is the more beautiful of the two options, however, it is a much tougher: in fact, it involves some of the most challenging walk

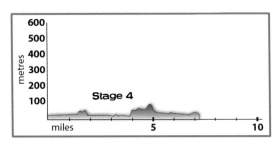

The view from Inversnaid Hotel (Stage 4/5a)

the entire trek. The path is often narrow, winding and covered with
ots and rocks, which are slippery when wet. After rain, it can be muddy.
quently, the path undulates relentlessly and is very tiring. The High
ute, on the other hand, takes advantage of a track which is much easier
hike. If you wish to head to Rowchoish Bothy then take the Low Route.

f Ptarmigan Lodge (①), wild camping is permitted: the land S of the
ge is within a LLTNP CMZ so wild camping is prohibited. Inversnaid
tel has a lovely location but it can be a busy place, often catering to
ge groups. Inversnaid Bunkhouse and Garrison of Inversnaid B&B are
ut 1 mile E of the hotel but you will have to climb the road (or one of
paths) to get there. Camping is permitted at the bunkhouse but there
so a specifically allocated wild camping area, right on the WHW, a few
utes N of Inversnaid Hotel along Stage 5a.

vardennan Hotel also has a beautiful location right next to the loch and
elcoming pub, the Clansman Bar. Rowardennan Lodge Youth Hostel
Ben Lomond Bunkhouse are right beside the WHW (about 0.5 miles N
owardennan).

route is generally well marked and navigation is usually straightforward.
vever, pay attention on the section between Rowardennan Hotel and
vardennan Lodge Youth Hostel: there are few waymarks.

	Time	Distance	Ascent S-N	Descent S-N
ge 4 Rowardennan/ Inversnaid	4:00	7.3miles 11.8km	653ft 199m	666ft 203m

Supplies/Water:

Rowardennan Lodge Youth Hostel (0.5 miles N of Rowardennan) – shop (basic provisions, confectionery and drinks)

Honesty box near Ben Lomond Bunkhouse – drinks & snacks

Refreshments/Food:

Rowardennan (Stage 3d/4) - Clansman Bar at Rowardennan Hotel

Rowardennan Lodge Youth Hostel (0.5 miles N of Rowardennan on Stage 4)

Inversnaid Hotel (Stage 4/5a)

Top Bunk Bistro at Inversnaid Bunkhouse (Stage 4/5a; 0.8 miles OR)

Loch Lomond (Stage 4)

Accommodation:

Rowardennan Hotel (Stage 3d/4)

Rowardennan Lodge Youth Hostel & Ben Lomond Bunkhouse (0.5 miles N of Rowardennan)

Rowchoish Bothy (Stage 4; Low Route)

Inversnaid Hotel (Stage 4/5a)

Inversnaid Bunkhouse (Stage 4/5a; 0.8 miles OR)

Garrison of Inversnaid B&B (Stage 4/5a; 1.1 miles OR)

Escape/Access:

Rowardennan (Stage 3d/4) – ferry/water-taxi

Inversnaid (Stage 4/5a) – ferry/water-taxi

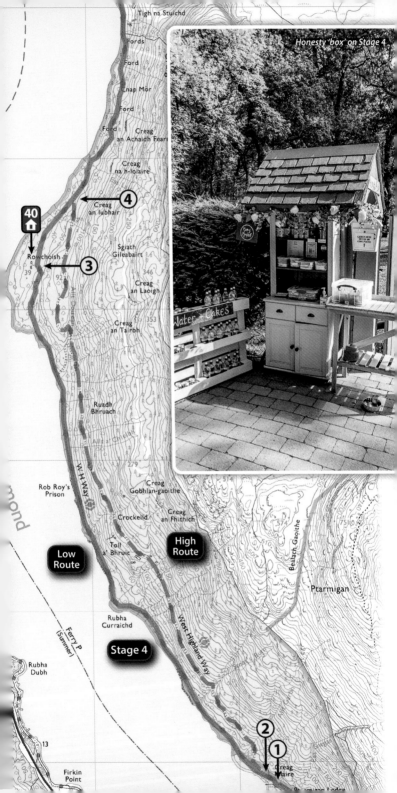

Tigh na Stuichd
Fords
Ford
Cnap Mòr
Ford
Ford
Creag
an Achaidh Fearr
Creag
na h-Iolaire
④ Creag an Iubhair
40 🏠
Rowchoish
③
Sgiath
Gileabairt
Creag
an Laoigh
Creag
an Tairbh
Ruadh
Bhruach
W.H.Way
Low Route
Rob Roy's Prison
Creag
Gobhlan-gaoithe
Creag
an Fhithich
Crockeild
High Route
Toll
a' Bhruic
Bealach Gaoithe
Ptarmigan
Rubha
Curraichd
Ferry P.
(Summer)
Stage 4
West Highland Way
Rubha
Dubh
13
Firkin
Point
②
①
Creag
Honesty 'box' on Stage 4
Water + Cakes

S-N

Stage 4: Rowardennan to Inversnaid

S From the **Clansman Bar**, keep SH on a path alongside the road. Soon, follow a path around the right side of a car park: later it becomes a track. Shortly after the access lane for **Rowardennan Lodge Youth Hostel**, TL at a fork. Shortly afterwards, pass **Ben Lomond Bunkhouse** and then an **honesty box**. Just afterwards, pass the **Ptarmigan Path** on the right, which leads to the summit of **Ben Lomond**: for directions to the summit, see www.walkhighlands.co.uk.

1 0:55: The **LLTNP CMZ** ends: wild camping is permitted N of this point.

2 1:00: Arrive at a junction. For the main WHW (**Low Route**), TL and descend on a path through trees. For the easier **High Route**, keep SH and stay on the track until **4**.

3 2:50: Arrive at a junction. TL for **Rowchoish Bothy** or keep SH to continue on Stage 4.

4 3:00: TL onto a track: this is where the High Route and Low Route meet again.

5 3:45: The path bends right and climbs alongside a gully with a beautiful waterfall. Just after crossing a bridge, TL and descend.

4:00: Arrive at **Inversnaid Hotel**.

N-S

Stage 4: Inversnaid to Rowardennan

From **Inversnaid Hotel**, climb E alongside a gully with a beautiful waterfall. Cross two footbridges and then descend along the S side of the gully.

0:15: The path bends left and follows the loch's shoreline.

1:00: Reach a junction. TR on a path for the main WHW (**Low Route**): alternatively, for the **High Route**, keep SH on the track until **2**.

1:10: Arrive at a junction. TR for **Rowchoish Bothy** or keep SH to continue on Stage 4.

3:00: TR onto a track: this is where the High Route and Low Route meet again.

3:05: The **LLTNP CMZ** begins: wild camping is not permitted S of this point. Pass the **Ptarmigan Path** on the left, which leads to the summit of **Ben Lomond**: for directions to the summit, see www.walkhighlands.co.uk. Just afterwards, pass an honesty box and then **Ben Lomond Bunkhouse**. Shortly afterwards, pass the access lane for **Rowardennan Lodge Youth Hostel**. Eventually, the track leads to a path running around the left of a car park. Soon, continue alongside a road.

4:00: Reach the **Clansman Bar** at **Rowardennan Hotel**

Inversnaid Hotel (Stage 4/5a)

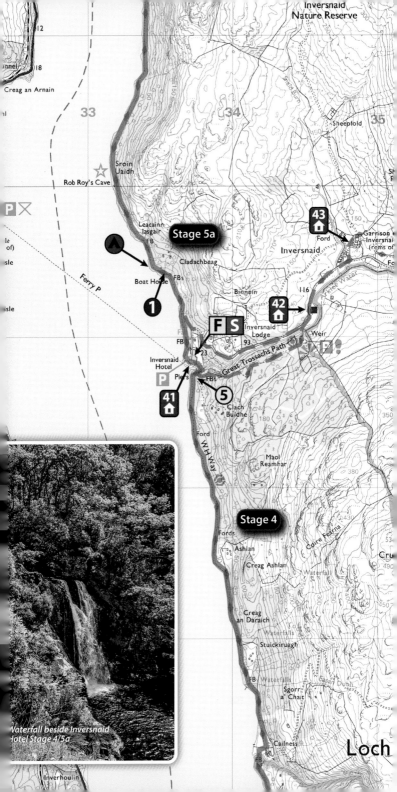

Inversnaid
Nature Reserve

Creag an Arnain

Sheepfold

Rob Roy's Cave

Sroin
Uaidh

Leacainn
Iasgair

Stage 5a

Garrison
Inversnai
(rems of

43

Ford

Cladachbeag

Inversnaid

Boat House

1

Binnein

116

42

Inversnaid
Lodge

F S

Weir

Great Trossachs Path

Inversnaid
Hotel

Piers

FBs

41

5

Clach
Buidhe

Maol
Reamhar

Stage 4

Fords

Ashlan

Creag Ashlan

Creag
an Daraich

Stuickiruagh

Cailness

Loch

Inverhoulin

Waterfall beside Inversnaid Hotel Stage 4/5a

5 Inversnaid/Inverarnan

A magnificent journey alongside Loch Lomond's most northerly shore For N-S trekkers, Section 5 will provide the first taste of Loch Lomon and it will be a sweet one. S-N trekkers, however, will leave the loch behir towards the end of the day but most will agree that the best loch-si scenery has been reserved until last: the forest alongside this part of Lo Lomond is punctuated with broad clearings, offering some of the fine views on the WHW. There are some tiring climbs but you will quickly forg your exertions at the superb vantage points. N of Cnap Mor, the path tak you along the beautiful Glen Falloch.

Ardlui Holiday Park (Stage 5a/5b; OR) has a superb location on the W sho of Loch Lomond. You can access it by ferry from Ardleish (Stage 5a/5b): soon as you arrive at a mast, raise the ball to summon the ferry (which v come at the next scheduled time). Ferry times are posted at the mast: s also www.ardlui.com.

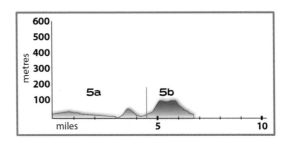

Descending towards Doune Byre Bothy (Stage 5a)

...inglas Farm Campsite at Inverarnan is right on the WHW: the grassy ...mp-ground is lovely and the restaurant, bar and shop are excellent. You ...n also stay at the nearby Drovers' Inn which is supposedly one of the ...ost haunted hotels in GB: even if you are not brave enough to spend the ...ght there, the pub is worth a visit. Wild camping is permitted on Section ... except in the Glen Falloch CMZ (which extends for a short distance ...ther side of Inverarnan: Stages 5b and 6a).

...versnaid Hotel has a lovely location but it can be a busy place, often ...tering to large groups. Inversnaid Bunkhouse and Garrison of Inversnaid ...B are about 1 mile E of the hotel but you will have to climb the road (or ...e of the paths) to get there. Camping is permitted at the bunkhouse but ...ere is also a specifically allocated wild camping area, right on the WHW, ...ew minutes N of Inversnaid Hotel.

...e entire section is well marked and navigation is straightforward. Some ...ths are tricky underfoot with rocks and roots. There are a few longer ...mbs.

		Time	Distance	Ascent W-E	Descent W-E
tage 5a	Inversnaid/Ardleish	1:45	4.5miles 7.2km	230ft 70m	200ft 61m
tage 5b	Ardleish/Inverarnan	1:15	2.2miles 3.5km	358ft 109m	404ft 123m

Supplies/Water:

Inverarnan (Stage 5b/6a) – shop at Beinglas Farm Campsite (groceries & gas canisters)

Refreshments/Food:

Inversnaid Hotel (Stage 4/5a)

Top Bunk Bistro at Inversnaid Bunkhouse (Stage 4/5a; 0.8 miles OR)

Ardlui Holiday Park (Stage 5a/5b; OR; access by ferry from Ardleish)

Inverarnan (Stage 5b/6a) – Beinglas Farm Restaurant; Drovers' Inn

The incredible view of Loch Lomond from Cnap Mor (Stage 5b)

Accommodation:

Inversnaid Hotel (Stage 4/5a)

Inversnaid Bunkhouse (Stage 4/5a; 0.8 miles OR)

Garrison of Inversnaid B&B (Stage 4/5a; 1.1 miles OR)

Wild camping area (Stage 5a) – 5-10min N of Inversnaid Hotel; camp-fires prohibited

Doune Byre Bothy (Stage 5a)

Ardlui Holiday Park (Stage 5a/5b; OR; access by ferry from Ardleish) – hotel, self-catering lodges & campsite

Inverarnan (Stage 5b/6a) – inn, campsite & B&B

Escape/Access:

Inversnaid (Stage 4/5a) – ferry/water-taxi

Ardleish (Stage 5a/5b) - ferry

Inverarnan (Stage 5b/6a) – bus

S-N

Stage 5a: Inversnaid to Ardleish

S From the N side of **Inversnaid Hotel's** car park, head N on a path, alongside the loch.

1 0:10: TL at a fork. Just afterwards, there is a superb **wild camping area**. The uneven path undulates and is quite tiring.

2 1:15: Just after crossing an open grassy area, the path bends right (away from the loch).

3 1:30: Pass **Doune Byre Bothy**. Afterwards, descend steeply back to the loch shore.

F 1:45: Cross a stile. Immediately afterwards, TL for the ferry to **Ardlui** or keep SH to start **Stage 5b**.

Stage 5b: Ardleish to Inverarnan

S Climb N on a path.

1 0:30: After a long climb, pass **Cnap Mor**: a short distance to the left of the path, there is an amazing **viewpoint**.

2 1:00: Enter a **LLTNP CMZ**: wild camping is prohibited N of this point (until the CMZ ends a short distance N of Inverarnan).

F 1:15: Arrive at **Beinglas Farm Campsite**. For the **Drovers' Inn**, pass to the left of the campsite restaurant and follow the farm access lane to a road: then TL along the road.

N-S

Stage 5b: Inverarnan to Ardleish

F From the S side of the campsite, head S on a path.

2 0:15: Leave the **LLTNP CMZ**: wild camping is permitted S of this point.

1 0:40: After a long climb, pass **Cnap Mor**: a short distance to the right of the path, there is an amazing **viewpoint** above Loch Lomond. Afterwards, descend S.

S 1:15: Reach a stile: TR for the ferry to **Ardlui** or keep SH (and cross the stile) to start **Stage 5a**.

Stage 5a: Ardleish to Inversnaid

F Cross the stile and continue S on a path. Soon start to climb.

3 0:20: Pass **Doune Byre Bothy** and continue climbing.

2 0:35: Cross an open grassy area and then continue S. The uneven path undulates and is quite tiring.

1 1:35: Pass a superb **wild camping area** and continue S.

S 1:45: Arrive at **Inversnaid Hotel**.

Doune Byre Bothy (Stage 5a)

Cnap Mòr

Loch

Outdoor
Centre   Pillars

Stage 5b

15

Pontoons

45

Hotel

Pier **Ardlui**

Marina

Ferry P
(Summer)

MS
Garristück

Landing
Stage

Burnside
Cottage

Railway
Cottage   21

A82

Cairn
Stuckendroin

Sheepfold

Ford

Ardleish

Ford

F **S**

FB

Fords

Ford

Ford

Ford

Fords

Doune

3

44

Loch
Lomond

Creag a'
Mhadaidh

Tarbh
Rock

Ford

2

FBs

Smug
Ca

Stage 5a

Creag a'
Phuint

Rubha
Ban

Island
I Vow

Castle
(remains of)

Ford

Ceann Mòr

West Highland Way

Ford

Pollochro

Tom na
h-Innse

MS

Footbridge on Stage 5a

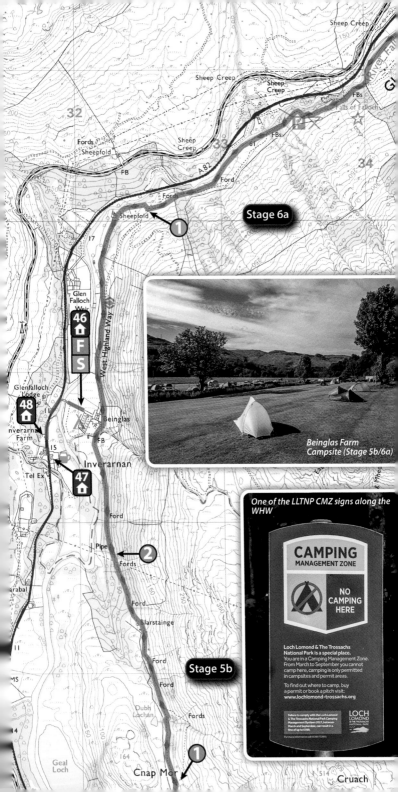

Stage 6a

Sheep Creep

River Fal

Sheep Creep

Sheep Creep

Falls of Falloch

FBs

FBs

A 82

Ford

Fords

Sheepfold

FB

Sheepfold

Fords

32

33

34

Glen Falloch Weir

West Highland Way

46 🏠 F S

48 🏠

nverarnan Farm

Glenfalloch Lodge

Tel Ex

47 🏠

Beinglas

FB

Inverarnan

Ford

Pipe

Fords

Ford

Blarstainge

Ford

Ford

Dubh Lochan

Fords

Geal Loch

Cnap Mor

Cruach

Stage 5b

Beinglas Farm Campsite (Stage 5b/6a)

One of the LLTNP CMZ signs along the WHW

CAMPING
MANAGEMENT ZONE

NO CAMPING HERE

Loch Lomond & The Trossachs National Park is a special place.
You are in a Camping Management Zone. From March to September you cannot camp here, camping is only permitted in campsites and permit areas.

To find out where to camp, buy a permit or book a pitch visit:
www.lochlomond-trossachs.org

Failure to comply with the Loch Lomond & The Trossachs National Park Camping Management Byelaws 2017, between March and September, can result in a fine of up to £500.

For more information call 01389 722031

LOCH LOMOND & THE TROSSACHS NATIONAL PARK

roaching the N end of
Lomond (Stage 5b)

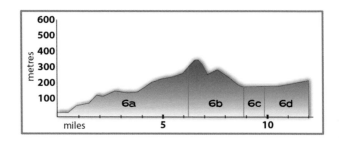

6 Inverarnan/Tyndrum

This is one of the most varied sections of the WHW. The route betwe
Inverarnan and Crianlarich along Glen Falloch (Stage 6a) is clas
highland terrain: rolling grassy slopes, surrounded by impressively rugg
summits. Between Crianlarich and Ewich House (Stage 6b), you delve i
forest. And finally, on Stages 6c and 6d, there are farmland and riversi
paths to enjoy, always in sight of the magnificent mountains. There is plei
of history too: SE of Strathfillan, Kirkton Burial Ground (with its 7th/8
century relics) and St. Fillan's Priory (13th century) are fascinating. You a
pass the site of the Battle of Dalrigh (see page 112). The only negative n
is the slightly irksome sight of the electricity pylons along Glen Fallo
fortunately, there are plans to replace the pylons with underground cab
in the near future.

Crianlarich is not the most attractive settlement on the WHW but i
roughly halfway along the trek and has a good shop where you can sto
up on supplies. There are also plenty of places to stay and eat. Tyndr
is probably a nicer place although it can be very busy: there are sho
restaurants and a variety of accommodation options. Both places also h

od transport links as they are on the Fort William/Glasgow train line. ‾athfillan Wigwam Village (Stage 6c/6d) is a lovely place to stay and it has hop where you can buy food and BBQ packs.

ld camping is not permitted in the Glen Falloch CMZ (which extends for ‾hort distance either side of Inverarnan: Stages 6a and 5b). Beinglas Farm ‾mpsite at Inverarnan is right on the WHW: the grassy camp-ground is ‾ely and the restaurant, bar and shop are excellent. You can also stay at ‾e nearby Drovers' Inn.

‾e section is well marked and navigation is straightforward. Between ‾erarnan and the Crianlarich exit, the WHW uses broad tracks, one of ‾ich is an old military road. Between Crianlarich and Tyndrum, there is a ‾xture of woodland paths, tracks and lanes.

		Time	Distance	Ascent S-N	Descent S-N
‾age 6a	Inverarnan/ Crianlarich exit	3:00(S-N) 2:30(N-S)	6.2miles 9.9km	942ft 287m	164ft 50m
‾age 6b	Crianlarich exit/ Ewich House	1:15(S-N) 1:30(N-S)	2.6miles 4.2km	463ft 141m	722ft 220m
‾age 6c	Ewich House/ Strathfillan	0:15	1.0miles 1.6km	43ft 13m	16ft 5m
‾age 6d	Strathfillan/ Tyndrum	1:00	2.2miles 3.5km	197ft 60m	46ft 14m

Supplies/Water:

Inverarnan (Stage 5b/6a) – shop at Beinglas Farm Campsite (groceries & gas canisters)

Crianlarich (Stage 6a/6b; 1 mile OR) – Crianlarich Store (groceries, gas canisters, walking gear & ATM); small shop at Crianlarich Youth Hostel (basic provisions, confectionery and drinks)

The Trading Post at Strathfillan Wigwam Village (Stage 6c/6d) – food & BBQ kits

Tyndrum (Stage 6d/7a) – shop at Pine Trees Camping Park (groceries & gas canisters); The Green Welly Stop (outdoor gear, gas cannisters, groceries, sandwiches, drinks & ATM); Brodies Mini Market (groceries)

Refreshments/Food:

Inverarnan (Stage 5b/6a) – Beinglas Farm Restaurant; Drovers' Inn

Crianlarich (Stage 6a/6b; 1 mile OR) – Rod & Reel pub; Crianlarich Hotel; Ben More Lodge; Station Tea Room

Strathfillan Wigwam Village (Stage 6c/6d) – bacon sandwiches available all day

Artisan Café (Stage 6d; 0.3 miles OR)

Tyndrum (Stage 6d/7a) – The Green Welly Stop; TJ's Diner, Tyndrum Inn; Real Food Café

*Approaching Strathfillan
(Stage 6c)*

Accommodation:

Inverarnan (Stage 5b/6a) – inn, campsite & B&B
Crianlarich (Stage 6a/6b; 1 mile OR) – hotels, B&Bs and youth hostel
Ewich House (Stage 6b/6c)
Strathfillan Wigwam Village (Stage 6c/6d)
Tyndrum (Stage 6d/7a) – hotels, B&Bs & camping

Escape/Access:

Inverarnan (Stage 5b/6a) – bus
Crianlarich (Stage 6a/6b; 1 mile OR) – bus/train
Tyndrum (Stage 6d/7a) – bus/train

S-N

Stage 6a: Inverarnan to Crianlarich exit

S From the E side of the campsite, head N on a gravel track.

1 0:25: TR on a path (easy to miss).

2 1:10: Cross a bridge: at the date of press, the bridge had been removed and the WHW was diverted. The diversion climbs to another bridge and then descends on a track back to the original route (adding 0.3 miles).

3 1:25: TL at a junction. 5min later, TL just after a cottage and cross a bridge. Shortly afterwards, TR on a path.

4 2:00: Pass through a low tunnel under the railway. Shortly afterwards, TR along a disused road. Soon, keep SH on a path. Then go through another tunnel and climb steeply.

F 3:00: Go through a gate to reach a junction. TR for the **Crianlarich Detour** (see box) or TL to start **Stage 6b**.

Stage 6b: Crianlarich exit to Ewich House

S From the junction, head W on a path, climbing through forest.

1 0:55: TL onto a path and climb: you may find paths heading more directly from this point to Ewich House, but at the date of press, they were obscured due to forestry works. 5min later, cross a track and descend on a path.

2 1:10: Pass under a railway bridge. Immediately afterwards, TL on a path.

F 1:15: Arrive at a road: TR along it for **Ewich House** (0.3 miles) or cross it to start **Stage 6c**.

Crianlarich Detour (1 mile; 15-20min)

From the junction, head E on a path. Descend through forest to the train station: pass under the tracks to head to **Crianlarich village centre**. Return to the WHW by the same route.

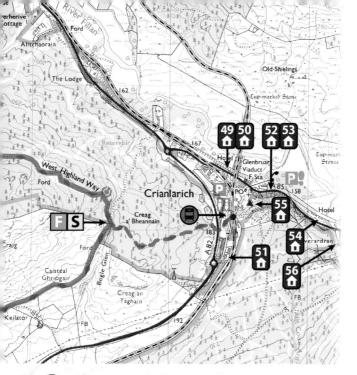

N-S

Stage 6b: Ewich House to Crianlarich exit

F Cross the road and pick up a path.

2 0:05: TR and pass under a railway bridge. Then climb on a path through forest. Cross a track.

1 0:25: After descending briefly, TR and climb on a path: you may find paths heading more directly to this point from Ewich House but, at the date of press, they were obscured due to forestry works.

S 1:30: Reach a junction beside a wooden fence. Head E for the **Crianlarich Detour** (see box) or TR and head SW to start **Stage 6a**.

Stage 6a: Crianlarich exit to Inverarnan

From the junction, go through a gate and head SW on a path. After 40min, descend steeply. Go through a tunnel. Keep SH along a disued road.

0:45: Soon TL and shortly afterwards, go through a low tunnel under the railway. After a while, TL and cross a bridge. Afterwards, TR and climb on a path.

1:15: TR at a junction. 5min later, keep SH at a junction: at the date of press, a diversion was in place and WHW trekkers had to TL at the junction. The diversion climbs to a bridge and then descends on a path back to the original route at **2** (adding 0.3 miles).

1:30: Cross a bridge.

2:10: TL onto a track.

2:30: Arrive at **Beinglas Farm Campsite**. For the **Drovers' Inn**, pass to the left of the campsite restaurant and follow the farm access lane to a road: then TL along the road.

Stage 7a

The Battle of Dalrigh

In 1306, at Dalrigh, Robert the Bruce was defeated in battle by Clan MacDougall (allies of the English). Bruce's army was crushed but he evaded capture, becoming a wanted fugitive. Legend states that, after the battle, Bruce and his remaining troops threw their weapons (including Bruce's long-sword) into the nearby **Lochan of the Lost Sword**. In 2015, a team from Macdonald Armouries in Edinburgh used metal detectors to search for the weapons but they found nothing.

S-N

Stage 6c: Ewich House to Strathfillan

S Cross the road. A few minutes later, TR and cross a bridge over the **River Fillan**.

1 0:05: TL just before a farm. Shortly afterwards, TL at **Kirkton Burial Ground**: four stone slabs carved with religious crosses (dating from the 7th/8th century) were found here and one of them is still visible. Just afterwards, pass the ruins of **St. Fillan's Priory** (13th century).

F 0:15: Arrive at **Strathfillan Wigwam Village**.

Stage 6d: Strathfillan to Tyndrum

S Head W from the **Trading Post shop** and cross a bridge. Immediately afterwards, TL on a lane. After 5min, TL onto a path and pass under the **A82**.

1 0:15: Cross a lane: alternatively, TL for the **Artisan Café**. 5min later, pass the site of the **Battle of Dalrigh**: see box. A few minutes later, TR onto a track. Just afterwards, keep SH past a bridge. Shortly afterwards, TL on a path.

2 0:30: Keep SH on a track. 5min later, TR and climb on a path. Shortly, pass the **Lochan of the Lost Sword**: see box.

3 0:50: Go through a gate. Just afterwards, TL at a junction. 5min later, keep SH at a junction: alternatively, TR across a bridge for **Pine Trees Camping Park**.

F 1:00: Reach a junction: TR to head into **Tyndrum** (5min) or TL to continue on the WHW or to head to the **Tyndrum Lower train station**. If you are not staying in Tyndrum and simply wish to resupply, it is quicker to TL because the WHW route soon passes **Brodies Mini Market**.

Stage 6d: Tyndrum to Strathfillan

F From the junction, head SE on a path. 5min later, keep SH at a junction: alternatively, TL across a bridge for **Pine Trees Camping Park**.

3 0:10: Go through a gate. Just afterwards, TL at a junction. 15min later, pass the **Lochan of the Lost Sword**: see box. Shortly afterwards, TL on a track.

2 0:30: 5min later, keep SH on a path. 5min later, pass the site of the **Battle of Dalrigh**: see box.

1 0:45: Cross a lane: alternatively, TR for the **Artisan Café**. Pass under the **A82** and then TR on a lane. 5min later, TR across a bridge.

S 1:00: Shortly afterwards, arrive at **Strathfillan Wigwam Village**.

Stage 6c: Strathfillan to Ewich House

F Head SE from the **Trading Post shop**.

1 0:10: Pass the ruins of **St. Fillan's Priory** (13th century). Just afterwards, TR at **Kirkton Burial Ground**: four stone slabs carved with religious crosses were found here (dating from the 7th/8th century) and one of them is still visible. Shortly afterwards, TR on a lane. Cross a bridge over the **River Fillan**. Immediately afterwards, TL.

S 0:15: A few minutes later, reach a road: TL along it for **Ewich House** (0.3 miles) or cross it to start **Stage 6b**.

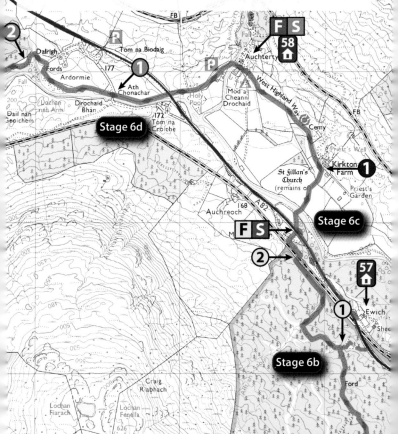

7 Tyndrum/Inveroran

Views of Beinn Dòrain
(Stage 7a)

This is one of the most iconic sections of the WHW. On Stage 7a, betwee
Tyndrum and Bridge of Orchy, the views of Beinn Dòrain (and a host
other summits) are sublime. And Stage 7b leads you to a lofty perch on th
NE slopes of Ben Inverveigh, directly above the beautiful Loch Tulla: th
panorama is unforgettable.

Bridge of Orchy Hotel (Stage 7a/7b) is a great place for an overnight sto
or a bite to eat: although it is located right next to the A82, the views a
fabulous. Inveroran Hotel (Stage 7b/8a) is one of the most memorab
lodgings on the entire trek: book well in advance. Its setting is wonderf
and the food and beer are excellent. There are also two magnificent wi
camping spots on this section: one is close to Bridge of Orchy Hotel a

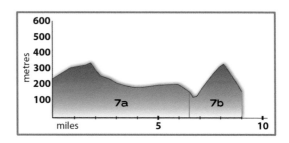

...e other is near Inveroran Hotel, enabling campers to dine at the hotels ...efore retiring to their tents.

...t Tyndrum, there are shops, restaurants and a variety of accommodation ...ptions. S-N trekkers should note that, N of Tyndrum, there are no shops ...ntil Kinlochleven (Stage 9/10a). Tyndrum & Bridge of Orchy are stops on ...e Fort William/Glasgow train line.

...e section is well marked and navigation is straightforward. For most of ...is section, you travel an old military road: at times, you can still make out ...e original cobbles. Whichever direction you are walking, Stage 7b entails ...tiring climb and a knee-jerking descent: fortunately, the exquisite views ...ould take your mind off the challenges.

		Time	Distance	Ascent S-N	Descent S-N
Stage 7a	Tyndrum/ Bridge of Orchy	2:45(S-N) 3:00(N-S)	6.5miles 10.5km	364ft 111m	564ft 172m
Stage 7b	Bridge of Orchy/ Inveroran	1:15	2.5miles 4.0km	535ft 163m	499ft 152m

Supplies/Water:

Tyndrum (Stage 6d/7a) – shop at Pine Trees Camping Park (groceries & gas canisters); The Green Welly Stop (outdoor gear, gas cannisters, groceries, sandwiches, drinks & ATM); Brodies Mini Market (groceries)

Refreshments/Food:

Tyndrum (Stage 6d/7a) – The Green Welly Stop; TJ's Diner, Tyndrum Inn; Real Food Café

Bridge of Orchy (Stage 7a/7b) – Bridge of Orchy Hotel; West Highland Way Sleeper (evening meals if booked in advance)

Inveroran Hotel (Stage 7b/8a)

Accommodation:

Tyndrum (Stage 6d/7a) – hotels, B&Bs & camping

Bridge of Orchy (Stage 7a/7b) – hotel, B&Bs and bunkhouse; wild camping area (beside the bridge over the River Orchy)

Inveroran (Stage 7b/8a) – Inveroran Hotel; wild camping area (5min W of Inveroran Hotel)

Escape/Access:

Tyndrum (Stage 6d/7a) – bus/train

Bridge of Orchy (Stage 7a/7b) – bus/train

The magnificent path between Bridge of Orchy and Inveroran (Stage 7b)

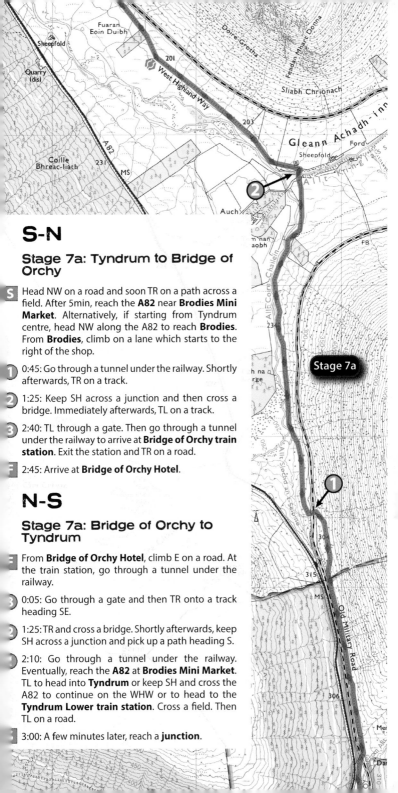

S-N

Stage 7a: Tyndrum to Bridge of Orchy

S Head NW on a road and soon TR on a path across a field. After 5min, reach the **A82** near **Brodies Mini Market**. Alternatively, if starting from Tyndrum centre, head NW along the A82 to reach **Brodies**. From **Brodies**, climb on a lane which starts to the right of the shop.

1 0:45: Go through a tunnel under the railway. Shortly afterwards, TR on a track.

2 1:25: Keep SH across a junction and then cross a bridge. Immediately afterwards, TL on a track.

3 2:40: TL through a gate. Then go through a tunnel under the railway to arrive at **Bridge of Orchy train station**. Exit the station and TR on a road.

F 2:45: Arrive at **Bridge of Orchy Hotel**.

N-S

Stage 7a: Bridge of Orchy to Tyndrum

F From **Bridge of Orchy Hotel**, climb E on a road. At the train station, go through a tunnel under the railway.

3 0:05: Go through a gate and then TR onto a track heading SE.

2 1:25: TR and cross a bridge. Shortly afterwards, keep SH across a junction and pick up a path heading S.

1 2:10: Go through a tunnel under the railway. Eventually, reach the **A82** at **Brodies Mini Market**. TL to head into **Tyndrum** or keep SH and cross the A82 to continue on the WHW or to head to the **Tyndrum Lower train station**. Cross a field. Then TL on a road.

S 3:00: A few minutes later, reach a **junction**.

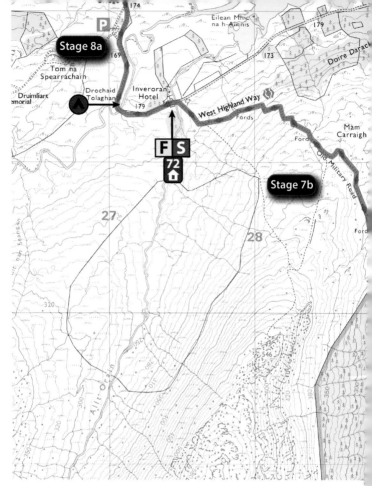

S-N

Stage 7b: Bridge of Orchy to Inveroran

S From **Bridge of Orchy Hotel**, descend W on a road. Soon cross a bridge: there is a lovely **wild camping area** on the W side of the bridge. Just afterwards, bear slightly right to pick up a path heading NW: ignore the lane to the right and the track to the left. After a long climb, descend to the NW.

F 1:15: TL along a lane and just afterwards, arrive at **Inveroran Hotel**.

N-S

Stage 7b: Inveroran to Bridge of Orchy

F From **Inveroran Hotel**, head NE on a lane. Shortly afterwards, TR and climb on a path which is an old military road. After a long climb, descend to the SE. Keep SH across a junction beside the **River Orchy** and cross a bridge: there is a lovely **wild camping area** on the W side of the bridge. Then climb E on a road.

S 1:15: Arrive at **Bridge of Orchy Hotel**.

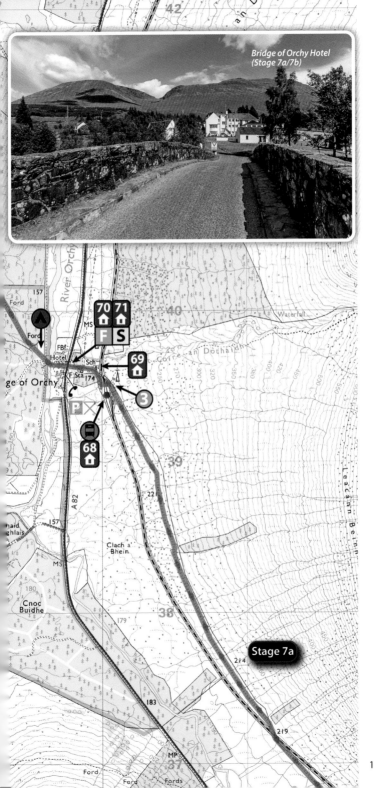

Bridge of Orchy Hotel (Stage 7a/7b)

Ford

157
Ford

River Orchy

Waterfall

40

MS

70 71
F S

FB
Hotel

Sch

Coire an Dothaidh

69

250 270 300 320 350 380 400 440 460 560 580

ge of Orchy

F Sta

174

3

P

68

39

A 82

220

Leacann Bheinn

157

haid
ghlais

MS

Clach a'
Bhein

180

179

38

Cnoc
Buidhe

Stage 7a

214

183

219

MP
37

Ford   Ford   Fords

This is probably the most remote part of the WHW: an old drove ro_
leads across Black Mount, a vast expanse of wild moorland just W
the inhospitable Rannoch Moor (one of the largest areas of uninhabit_
wilderness in GB). Other than the clear track upon which you walk, the_
are almost no signs of human habitation for much of the journey. Instea
you are surrounded by spectacular mountains, little lochs and seemin_
endless miles of heather. From the highpoint (445m), which is marked wi
a cairn, there are superb views over Rannoch Moor to the E. For S-N trekke_
the descent towards Kingshouse is the cherry on the cake, providing _
epic conclusion to an incredible day of hiking. SE of Kingshouse, look _
for the famous Blackrock Cottage which is one of the most photograph_
sights on the WHW. Pray for a clear day as this entire section is a highli_
of the trek.

There are good facilities at Glencoe Mountain Resort: at the date of pre_
the café was being re-built after a fire in 2019. Despite its name, Glen_
Mountain Resort is actually a short distance away from the valley of G_
Coe and it should not be confused with the village of Glencoe (which is _
miles further W and is not on the route of the WHW).

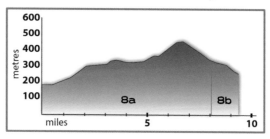

...he old Kingshouse Hotel, one of Scotland's oldest licensed inns, was a ...uch-loved Highland institution. In 2019, it reopened after substantial ...furbishment which apparently cost around £12.5 million: most of the ...uilding was demolished and a large modern hotel was constructed, ...ith the original 18th century parts being incorporated into it. The new ...uilding blends reasonably well into the magnificent surroundings and ...e facilities are now vastly improved. However, for the trekker, all this ...mes at a cost because food and lodging at the hotel are not cheap.

...veroran Hotel is one of the most memorable lodgings on the entire trek: ...ook well in advance. Its setting is wonderful and the food and beer are ...cellent. There is also a magnificent wild camping spot a short distance ...of the hotel.

...though the track used by the WHW is clear, well-marked and ...aightforward to navigate, in poor conditions or low visibility, the moor ...an intimidating place. In such conditions, be sure not to stray from the ...HW route.

		Time	Distance	Ascent S-N	Descent S-N
tage 8a	Inveroran/ Glencoe Mountain Resort exit	3:45(S-N) 3:30(N-S)	8.1miles 13.1km	843ft 257m	400ft 122m
tage 8b	Glencoe Mountain Resort exit/ Kingshouse	0:30(S-N) 0:45(N-S)	1.3miles 2.1km	33ft 10m	253ft 77m

Supplies/Water:

Tap at Kingshouse Hotel (stage 8b/9)

Refreshments/Food:

Inveroran Hotel (Stage 7b/8a)

Glencoe Mountain Resort (Stage 8a/8b) – new café under construction at date of press

Kingshouse Hotel (Stage 8b/9) – The Way Inn; Kingshouse Bar; Kingshouse Restaurant

Blackrock Cottage (Stage 8b)

Accommodation:

Inveroran (Stage 7b/8a) – Inveroran Hotel; wild camping area (5min W of Inveroran Hotel)

Glencoe Mountain Resort (Stage 8a/8b) – campsite & micro-lodges

Kingshouse Hotel (Stage 8b/9) – private rooms & bunkhouse

Escape/Access:

Glencoe (Stage 8b/9; 13 miles OR) - bus

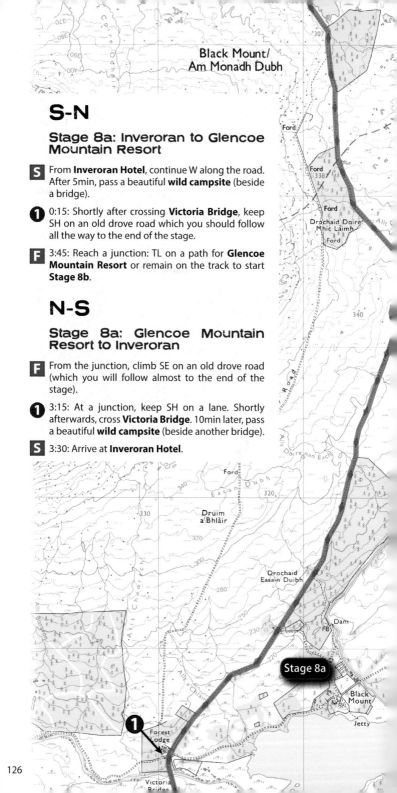

S-N

Stage 8a: Inveroran to Glencoe Mountain Resort

S From **Inveroran Hotel**, continue W along the road. After 5min, pass a beautiful **wild campsite** (beside a bridge).

1 0:15: Shortly after crossing **Victoria Bridge**, keep SH on an old drove road which you should follow all the way to the end of the stage.

F 3:45: Reach a junction: TL on a path for **Glencoe Mountain Resort** or remain on the track to start **Stage 8b**.

N-S

Stage 8a: Glencoe Mountain Resort to Inveroran

F From the junction, climb SE on an old drove road (which you will follow almost to the end of the stage).

1 3:15: At a junction, keep SH on a lane. Shortly afterwards, cross **Victoria Bridge**. 10min later, pass a beautiful **wild campsite** (beside another bridge).

S 3:30: Arrive at **Inveroran Hotel**.

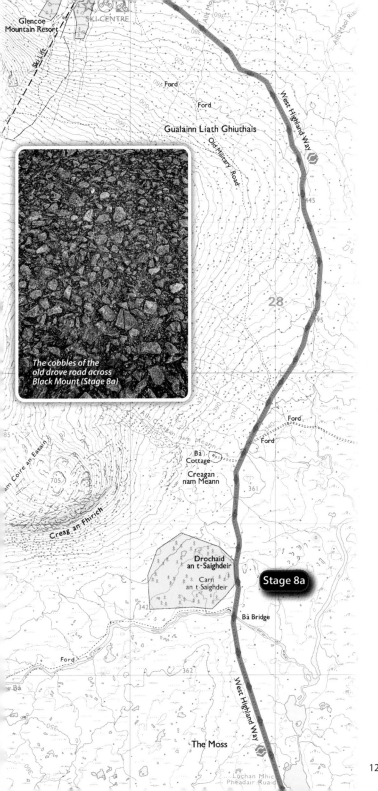

Glencoe
Mountain Resort

SKI CENTRE

Ford

Ford

West Highland Way

Gualainn Liath Ghiuthais

Old Military Road

445

*The cobbles of the
old drove road across
Black Mount (Stage 8a)*

28

395

Allt Creagan nam Meann

Ford

Ford

Bà
Cottage

Creagan
nam Meann

361

m Coire an Easain

705

Creag an Fhirich

Drochaid
an t-Saighdeir

Carn
an t-Saighdeir

Stage 8a

342

Bà Bridge

Ford

362

West Highland Way

The Moss

r Bà

350

Lochan Mhic
Pheadair Ruaidh

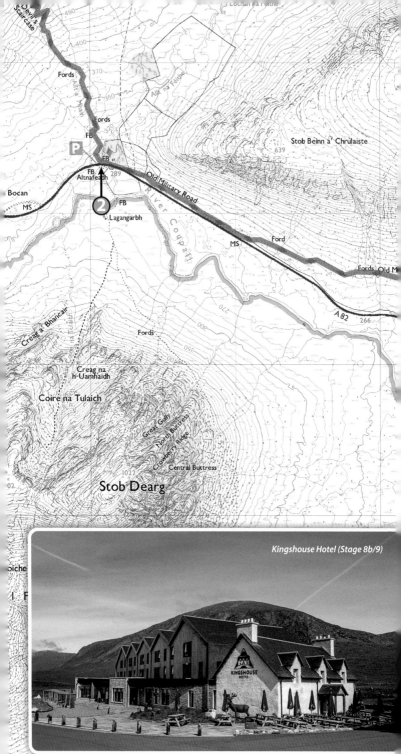

Kingshouse Hotel (Stage 8b/9)

S-N

Stage 8b: Glencoe Mountain Resort to Kingshouse

S From the junction, head N on the track. 5min later, at **Blackrock Cottage**, TR on a lane.

1 0:15: Cross the **A82** and head NW on a path.

F 0:30: Arrive at **Kingshouse Hotel**.

N-S

Stage 8b: Kingshouse to Glencoe Mountain Resort

F From **Kingshouse Hotel**, head SE on a path.

1 0:20: Cross the **A82** and head S on a lane. At **Blackrock Cottage**, TL on a path: alternatively, keep SH on the lane for **Glencoe Mountain Resort**.

S 0:40: Reach a junction. To start **Stage 8a**, keep SH on the path: the path on the right comes from **Glencoe Mountain Resort**.

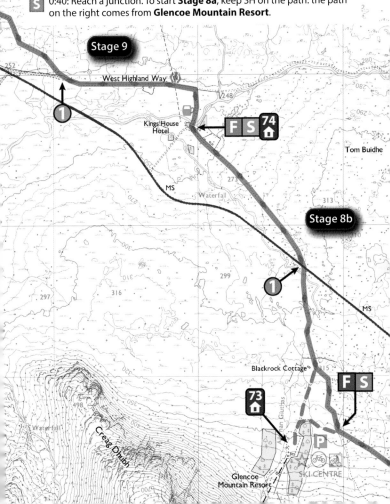

Kingshouse/ Kinlochleven

9

This sublime route is another highlight of the WHW. The scenery [is] exceptional throughout. Whichever direction you travel, the quali[ty] of the views intensifies as you gain altitude by climbing to the vanta[ge] point above the ominously named Devil's Staircase: at 548m, this is t[he] highest point on the WHW so take plenty of time to savour the exception[al] Highland panorama. Just W of Kingshouse Hotel, Glen Etive and Glen C[oe] are exquisite.

There is no accommodation mid-route. Fortunately, for S-N trekke[rs] there are plenty of places to stay in Kinlochleven (which also offers t[he] first opportunity for re-supply since Tyndrum). For N-S hikers, the or[ly] accommodation is at Kingshouse Hotel which books up quickly: if y[ou]

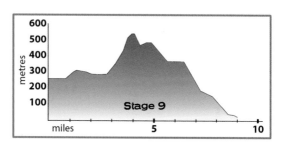

The route passes the summit of Buachaille Etive Mòr (Stage 9)

nnot secure a reservation at the hotel, the next accommodation is at
encoe Mountain Village (Stage 8b) or Inveroran (Stage 8a). N-S trekkers
ould note that, after leaving Kinlochleven, there are no shops until
ndrum (Stage 7a).

ere is a lot of climbing on this strenuous section, particularly for N-S
ekkers, for whom the difficulty is compounded by the fact that the
evious stage involved the equally tough route from Fort William. For S-N
ekkers, the climb of the Devil's Staircase is probably the most challenging
cent on the WHW, although it is fair to say that it is not as terror-inducing
its name would suggest: N-S trekkers should take care descending on
e steep, rocky path.

e section is generally well marked but take care with directions
proaching/leaving Kinlochleven where there is a labyrinth of paths
d tracks. Take great care in poor conditions or low visibility as this high
ountain route is very exposed.

		Time	Distance	Ascent S-N	Descent S-N
tage 9	Kingshouse/ Kinlochleven	4:30(S-N) 5:00(N-S)	8.9miles 14.3km	1221ft 372m	2001ft 610m

Supplies/Water:

Tap at Kingshouse Hotel (stage 8b/9)

Kinlochleven (Stage 9/10a) – supermarket; ATM

Refreshments/Food:

Kingshouse Hotel (Stage 8b/9) – The Way Inn; Kingshouse Bar; Kingshouse Restaurant

Kinlochleven (Stage 9/10a) – Tailrace Inn; Highland Getaway pub; Bothy Bar at MacDonald Hotel; Riverside Chippy

The incredible setting of Kingshouse Hotel (Stage 8b/9)

Accommodation:
Kingshouse Hotel (Stage 8b/9) – hotel & bunkhouse
Kinlochleven (Stage 9/10a) – hotel, B&Bs, bunkhouses & camping

Escape/Access:
Glencoe (Stage 8b/9; 13 miles OR) - bus
Kinlochleven (Stage 9/10a) - bus

S-N

Stage 9: Kingshouse to Kinlochleven

S From the hotel, head N on a lane. A few minutes later, TL at a junction.

1 0:15: TR onto a path.

2 1:20: The path bends right, climbing steeply away from the road. This is one of the toughest climbs on the WHW. Just to the W is the famously beautiful **Glen Coe**.

3 2:10: Keep SH across the top of the **Devil's Staircase (548m)** and start to descend. The views are exquisite.

4 3:30: TL down a track.

5 3:45: Cross a bridge and then climb.

6 4:25: TR and cross a bridge. Soon pass **Blackwater Hostel & Campsite**.

F 4:30: A few minutes later, arrive at the bridge in the centre of **Kinlochleven**.

N-S

Stage 9: Kinlochleven to Kingshouse

F From the bridge in the centre of **Kinlochleven**, follow a path along the S bank of the **River Leven**. A few minutes later, pass **Blackwater Hostel & Campsite**.

6 0:10: Cross a bridge over pipes. Then TL and climb on a path.

5 1:00: Cross a bridge and climb.

4 1:30: TR and climb on a path.

3 3:15: Keep SH across the top of the **Devil's Staircase (548m)**: the views are exquisite. Take care as you descend: the steep path is covered in loose rock.

2 3:45: At the **A82**, the path turns left. Just to the W is the famously beautiful **Glen Coe**.

1 4:45: TL on a lane. 10min later, TR at a junction.

S 5:00: Arrive at **Kingshouse Hotel**.

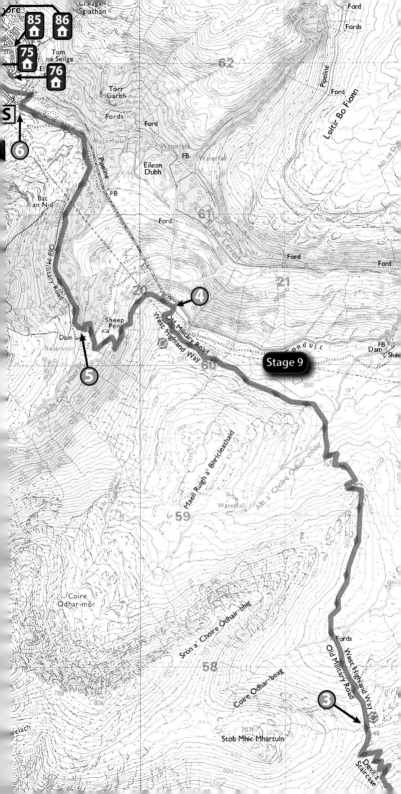

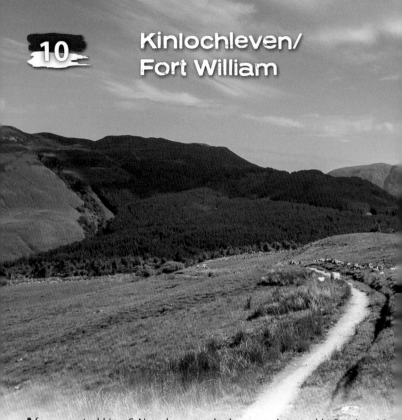

I f you are trekking S-N and you are lucky enough to tackle Section 10 o a fine day, it will seem that the WHW has saved the best until last. Th scenery is spectacular throughout but the seemingly never-ending gle NW of Kinlochleven is unforgettable: an easy path winds its way throug textbook Scottish slopes of grass and heather, hemmed in by mountains divine beauty. However, it is Ben Nevis that most walkers will be despera to see because, on this part of the WHW, the UK's highest mountain mak its most significant appearance: the entire northern half of Section is dominated by the 'Ben'. The summit is covered with cloud much mo often than not so pray for a clear day. Approaching Glen Nevis, recent tr felling has temporarily marred the scenery slightly. There is a silver lini though because the removal of the trees has enhanced the views of B Nevis as you pass through the forest.

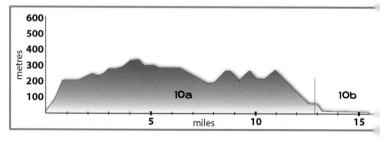

Ben Nevis showing herself on Stage 10a

ort William has a wide variety of places to stay. Its setting between Loch nnhe and Ben Nevis is spectacular but the town itself evokes mixed actions. It is hardly Scotland's most beautiful settlement but it is a easant place, having improved greatly in recent years. There are plenty f pubs and restaurants suitable for a post-trek celebration. There are also od and outdoor shops, making it an excellent place for N-S trekkers to ovision at the start of the WHW.

-S trekkers will also find plenty of accommodation options in Kinlochleven: ey should note that, after leaving Kinlochleven, there are no shops until ndrum (Stage 7a).

iis long, tough section is generally well marked but take care with rections approaching/leaving Kinlochleven where there is a labyrinth of aths and tracks. Take great care in poor conditions or low visibility as this a high mountain route.

		Time	Distance	Ascent W-E	Descent W-E
tage 10a	Kinlochleven/ Glen Nevis exit	6:30	12.9miles 20.7km	2024ft 617m	1887ft 575m
tage 10b	Glen Nevis exit/ Fort William	1:00	2.5miles 4.0km	16ft 5m	154ft 47m

Supplies/Water:

Kinlochleven (Stage 9/10a) – supermarket & ATM

Glen Nevis (Stage 10a/10b) - shop at Glen Nevis Caravan & Camping Park (basic groceries)

Fort William (Stage 10b) – shops, supermarkets, pharmacies & ATMs

Refreshments/Food:

Kinlochleven (Stage 9/10a) – Tailrace Inn; Highland Getaway pub; Bothy Bar at MacDonald Hotel; Riverside Chippy

Glen Nevis (Stage 10a/10b) - Ben Nevis Inn; Glen Nevis Restaurant & Bar at Glen Nevis Caravan & Camping Park

Fort William (Stage 10b) – pubs, restaurants & cafés

*Climbing the wonderful glen
NW of Kinlochleven (Stage 10a)*

Accommodation:

Kinlochleven (Stage 9/10a) – hotel, B&Bs, bunkhouses & camping

Glen Nevis (Stage 10a/10b) – B&Bs & camping

Fort William (Stage 10b) – hotels, B&Bs & hostel

Escape/Access:

Kinlochleven (Stage 9/10a) - bus

Glen Nevis (Stage 10a/10b) – bus

Fort William (Stage 10b) – bus/train

S-N

Stage 10a: Kinlochleven to Glen Nevis

S Head S across the bridge in the centre of **Kinlochleven**. Soon, pass the **Tailrace Inn**.

(1) 0:10: TR and climb on a path: alternatively, continue a short distance along the road to reach **MacDonald Hotel & Cabins**. Take care to follow WHW markings at any junctions: if in doubt, keep climbing.

(2) 1:00: TL onto a track and traverse the grassy slopes on an old military road which leads you deeper and deeper into a magnificent valley.

(3) 3:30: Just before a gate, TL onto a grassy path to head around a sheep enclosure. After it, return to the track.

(4) 4:00: Keep SH across a track and climb on a path. 15min later, TL at a junction, climbing on a narrow path. Soon the path travels lovely grassy slopes with magnificent views of **Ben Nevis**: this is a WHW highlight.

(5) 5:45: TR onto a track. A few minutes later, pass a path on the right which heads to the remains of **Dun Deardail Fort** (see page 144). Afterwards, descend on the track.

F 6:30: Reach a **junction**: TL to start **Stage 10b** or TR for **Glen Nevis Youth Hostel/ Glen Nevis Caravan & Camping Park**.

N-S

Stage 10a: Glen Nevis to Kinlochleven

F From the **junction**, climb S on a track. After a long climb, pass a path on the left which heads to the remains of **Dun Deardail Fort** (see page 144).

⑤ 1:20: A few minutes later, TL and descend on a path which soon undulates through forest with superb views of **Ben Nevis** to the NE. Later, the path travels lovely grassy slopes with more magnificent views of Ben Nevis: this is a WHW highlight.

④ 3:10: Keep SH across a track.

③ 3:40: TR onto a grassy path to head around a sheep enclosure. After it, return to the track which now climbs. Head over a rise and then descend an old military road through a magnificent valley.

② 5:55: TR and descend on a path. Take care to follow WHW markings at any junctions.

① 6:20: TL along a road: alternatively, TR for **MacDonald Hotel & Cabins**.

S 6:30: Shortly after the **Tailrace Inn**, reach the bridge in the centre of **Kinlochleven**.

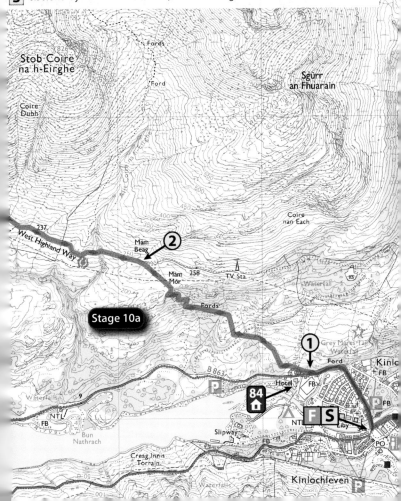

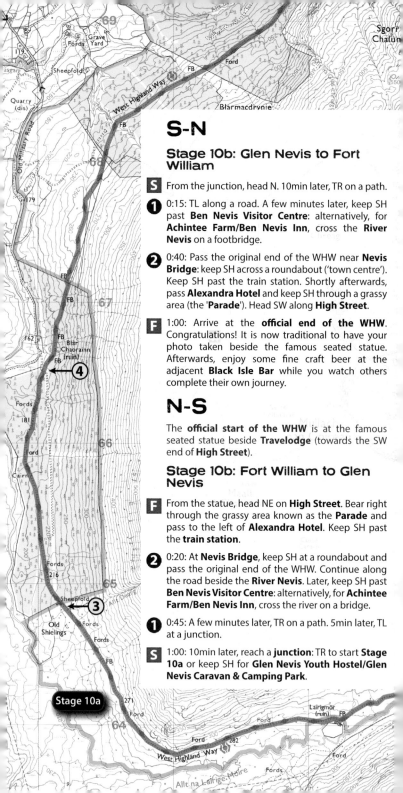

S-N

Stage 10b: Glen Nevis to Fort William

S From the junction, head N. 10min later, TR on a path.

1 0:15: TL along a road. A few minutes later, keep SH past **Ben Nevis Visitor Centre**: alternatively, for **Achintee Farm/Ben Nevis Inn**, cross the **River Nevis** on a footbridge.

2 0:40: Pass the original end of the WHW near **Nevis Bridge**: keep SH across a roundabout ('town centre'). Keep SH past the train station. Shortly afterwards, pass **Alexandra Hotel** and keep SH through a grassy area (the '**Parade**'). Head SW along **High Street**.

F 1:00: Arrive at the **official end of the WHW**. Congratulations! It is now traditional to have your photo taken beside the famous seated statue. Afterwards, enjoy some fine craft beer at the adjacent **Black Isle Bar** while you watch others complete their own journey.

N-S

The **official start of the WHW** is at the famous seated statue beside **Travelodge** (towards the SW end of **High Street**).

Stage 10b: Fort William to Glen Nevis

F From the statue, head NE on **High Street**. Bear right through the grassy area known as the **Parade** and pass to the left of **Alexandra Hotel**. Keep SH past the **train station**.

2 0:20: At **Nevis Bridge**, keep SH at a roundabout and pass the original end of the WHW. Continue along the road beside the **River Nevis**. Later, keep SH past **Ben Nevis Visitor Centre**: alternatively, for **Achintee Farm/Ben Nevis Inn**, cross the river on a bridge.

1 0:45: A few minutes later, TR on a path. 5min later, TL at a junction.

S 1:00: 10min later, reach a **junction**: TR to start **Stage 10a** or keep SH for **Glen Nevis Youth Hostel/Glen Nevis Caravan & Camping Park**.

Climbing Ben Nevis (5.5-9hr)

Ben Nevis (1344m) is the UK's highest mountain and climbing it is a fabulous way to finish your trip. However, for a number of reasons, the route to the summit is much more challenging than most people's daily endeavours on the WHW. Firstly, the summit is more than 1300m above the normal start points at **Ben Nevis Visitor Centre (BNVC)**, **Achintee Farm** and **Glen Nevis Youth Hostel**, all of which are right next to the route of the WHW. That is a long and challenging climb, even for fit and experienced hikers.

Secondly, for much of the year, the summit is covered in cloud and can be a dangerous place in low visibility or bad weather. Although the summit plateau is broad, in cloud or mist there are few visible landmarks to help you navigate back off the mountain: it is easy to get disorientated and there are dangerous drops and gullies, particularly to the N and SW of the plateau. Accordingly, although tens of thousands of people successfully climb the mountain each year, you should not attempt it unless you have sufficient fitness and hill-walking experience and you are properly equipped. Furthermore, you should never attempt to climb Ben Nevis if conditions are poor or if bad weather is forecast: make sure that you check the weather forecast before you start (see 'Weather'). You should also ensure that you have a map (**OS Sheet 392 Ben Nevis & Fort William**) and compass and know how to use them.

Most people climb on the '**Mountain Path**' (which used to be known as the 'Tourist Route') and start at BNVC: accordingly, this is the route that we describe here. You can also access the Mountain Path by starting from Achintee Farm or Glen Nevis Youth Hostel.

Directions

S From **BNVC**, cross a footbridge over the **River Nevis**. Immediately afterwards, TR. Shortly afterwards, TL at a sign. A few minutes later, cross a stile and keep SH. Shortly afterwards, TR at a junction onto the **Mountain Path** which climbs across the slopes of **Meall an t-Suidhe**: hikers starting from **Achintee Farm** will reach this junction on the path arriving from the N.

1 After a while, keep SH at a junction: hikers starting from **Glen Nevis Youth Hostel** will reach this junction on the path arriving from the right. After crossing some footbridges, the path climbs NE up the side of **Red Burn valley**: at the head of the valley, the path turns sharply left and zigzags up to a plateau near **Lochan Meall an t-Suidhe** (the 'Halfway Lochan').

2 Soon after the gradient increases again, TR at a junction. After crossing **Red Burn**, the path becomes rockier as it zigzags up the W slopes of the mountain.

3 Between 1100 and 1200m, pass **Five Finger Gully** on the right. In poor conditions, it is common for descending walkers to stray precariously close to this gully: it is therefore sensible to study the surrounding terrain now to ensure that you know how you will descend later on. As you approach the summit plateau, the gradient eases. You will pass close to two gullies to the N (firstly **Tower Gully** and then **Gardyloo Gully**). Shortly after **Gardyloo Gully**, arrive at the **summit of Ben Nevis (1344m)**. It is lovely to linger and savour the spectacular views but remember that you need to leave time to negotiate your way back down again.

To descend, follow the same route. In low visibility, take great care to avoid the gullies. From the trig point on the summit, follow a grid bearing of **231°** for a distance of **150m**. Then bear right and follow a grid bearing of **281°** across the summit plateau to meet the zigzags heading down the W slopes of the mountain. From there, retrace your steps to the start.

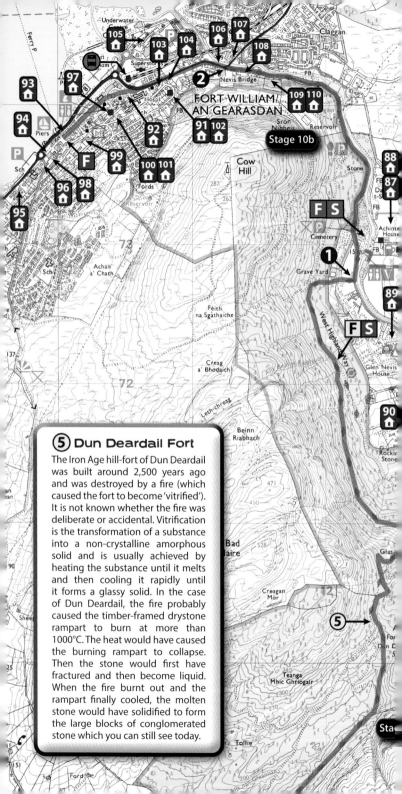

⑤ Dun Deardail Fort

The Iron Age hill-fort of Dun Deardail was built around 2,500 years ago and was destroyed by a fire (which caused the fort to become 'vitrified'). It is not known whether the fire was deliberate or accidental. Vitrification is the transformation of a substance into a non-crystalline amorphous solid and is usually achieved by heating the substance until it melts and then cooling it rapidly until it forms a glassy solid. In the case of Dun Deardail, the fire probably caused the timber-framed drystone rampart to burn at more than 1000°C. The heat would have caused the burning rampart to collapse. Then the stone would first have fractured and then become liquid. When the fire burnt out and the rampart finally cooled, the molten stone would have solidified to form the large blocks of conglomerated stone which you can still see today.

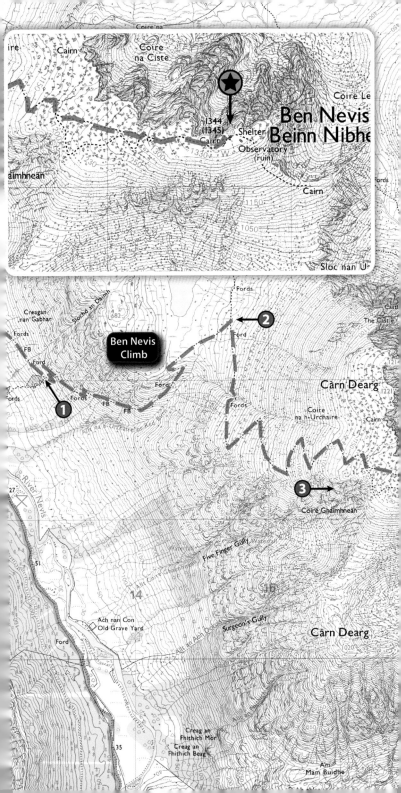

Views of Loch Tulla
(Stage 7b)

Notes

KNIFE EDGE
Outdoor Guidebooks

We thought guidebooks were boring so we decided to change them. Mapping is better than 40 years ago. Graphics are better than 40 years ago. Photography is better than 40 years ago. So why have walking guidebooks remained the same?

Well our guidebooks are **different**:

▶ **We use Real Maps.** You know, the **1:25,000/1:50,000** scale maps that walkers actually use to navigate with. Not sketch maps that get you lost. Real maps make more work for us but we think it is worth it. You do not need to carry separate maps and you are less likely to get lost so we save you time!

▶ **Numbered Waypoints** on our Real Maps link to the walk descriptions, making routes easier to follow than traditional text-based guidebooks. No more wading through pages of boring words to find out where you are! You want to look at incredible scenery and not have your face stuck in a book all day. Right?

▶ **Colour, colour, colour.** Mountains and cliffs are **beautiful** so guidebooks should be too. We were fed up using guidebooks which were ugly and boring. When planning, we want to be **dazzled** with full-size colour pictures of the **magnificence** which awaits us! So our guidebooks fill every inch of the page with beauty: big, **spectacular** photos of mountains, etc. Oh yeah baby!

▶ **More practical size.** Long and slim. Long enough to have Real Maps and large pictures but slim enough to fit in a pocket.

Now all that sounds great to us but we want to know if you like what we have done. So hit us with your feedback: good or bad. We are not too proud to change.

Follow us for trekking advice, book updates, discount coupons, articles and other interesting hiking stuff.

www.knifeedgeoutdoor.com

info@knifeedgeoutdoor.com

@knifeedgeoutdoor

@knifeedgeout

@knifeedgeoutdoor

Facebook Groups

If you have any questions which are not answered in our books, then you can ask the author in one of our Facebook Groups. Updates to our books can be found in the topic sections of the groups.

The group for this book is 'West Highland Way Q&A'. The group's URL is **www.facebook.com/groups/ WestHighlandWayTrek**